Hold It!

How to Sew Bags, Totes,
Duffels, Pouches, and More

OTHER BOOKS AVAILABLE FROM CHILTON
Robbie Fanning, Series Editor

Hold It!

How to Sew Bags, Totes, Duffels, Pouches, and More

by Nancy Restuccia

Chilton Book Company
Radnor, Pennsylvania

This book is dedicated to Dave and Danielle, who put up with me during my "bag lady" period.

Color-Plate Photography by
Frank Schneider

Book Design by
Nancy Restuccia

Illustrations by
Joan D. Johnson
& Nancy Restuccia

Cover Concept by
Nancy Restuccia

Cover Design by
Tony Jacobson

Samples sewn by
Nancy Restuccia

Published in Radnor, Pennsylvania, 19089, by Chilton Book Company

Manufactured in the United States of America

Library of Congress Cataloging-in-Publication Data:

Restuccia, Nancy.
    Hold it! : how to sew bags, totes, duffels, pouches, and more! / by Nancy Restuccia ; [color photographs by Frank Schneider ; illustrations by Joan D. Johnson & Nancy Restuccia].
        p. cm.
    ISBN 0-8019-8494-7 (pb)
    1. Bags. 2. Sewing. I. Title
TT667.R472 1994
646.2'1—dc20   93-48333
                                                                CIP

        6 7 8 9 0   3 2 1 0 9 8 7

Contents

Preface

Since the dawn of civilization, we have been carrying things; early on, we realized that bags could make the task easier. Bags appear in the earliest wall paintings from Neolithic times (6000–3500 B.C.) . . . in the stelae and relief carvings of early Mesopotamian cultures (3000–500 B.C.) . . . in the frescoes, sculptures, and pottery of the ancient Egyptians, Greeks, and Romans (3000 B.C.–A.D. 500). Most often, they are bags for carrying arrows and swords, food and water.

Today, bags are enjoying tremendous popularity and seemingly endless variety. There are still bags for archers and warriors, but they are now vastly outnumbered by bags for bikers, hikers, golfers, skiers, quilters, anglers, in-line skaters, weightlifters, gardeners, sailors, picnickers, travelers, and children. You name it, someone probably makes a bag for it.

And with the recent raising of our collective environmental consciousness, fabric shopping and lunch bags are finding particular favor as the reusable alternative to their throwaway paper predecessors. It's the right thing to do.

Along with their increasing variety and popularity, bags today are increasing in price. A recent issue of *Mirabella* magazine featured a selection of contemporary bags—most of them very simple in form, easily sewable—ranging in price from a "modest" $194 for a Coach shoulder bag to an impressive $1,170 for a silvered-leather duffel from Chanel. The latest Saks catalog offered a cotton canvas duffel for $650. At those prices, you can save yourself a small fortune by making them yourself. And if you can sew a straight seam, there's no reason you can't.

Introduction

Bags are easy to sew. Take it from me; I've made over a hundred of them in the past nine months.

They are also generally forgiving, so even a beginner can feel comfortable tackling the projects in this book. All that is really required is a straight-stitch sewing machine in good working order and a sharp, new needle. For certain bags and fabrics, it is helpful to have a zigzag-stitch capability, and sometimes a low-gear option, but these are not necessary.

I suspect that what has kept even the most experienced among us from venturing into this new sewing domain is the perception that appropriate fabrics and notions for bag making are hard to find. I assure you, they are readily available. Everything you need is, at most, a mail order away. And with the current popularity of making bags of all kinds, supplies and materials are becoming easier to find locally with each passing day.

How to Use This Book

Most bags can be categorized into a handful of basic shapes, and that is how this book is organized: Flat Bags, Totes, Duffels, Cases, and Rolls & Pouches. The characteristics of each form are described in the chapter introduction, followed by several specific projects based on that form.

Many of these projects conclude with an "Options, Ideas, & Variations . . . " section, which gives a number of possibilities for changing the basic bag form. Keep in mind, these possibilities are by no means exhaustive. My hope is that, by understanding the basic forms, you will be able to categorize any bag you see and be able to (1) make it yourself based on the instructions for that basic form or (2) improvise and come up with a new, different, totally customized bag that suits your own particular needs and desires.

Terms, Abbreviations, and Conventions

Many common (and some not-so-common) terms are used in this book to describe sewing procedures as well as materials and supplies that are peculiar to bag making. A few sewing abbreviations are used, too, mostly within the illustrations. If you are unfamiliar with a term or abbreviation, please consult the glossary (page 127) for a definition or explanation.

In the illustrations, shading is used to indicate the right side of fabric and white, the wrong side, following the conventions of the pattern industry.

The Four-Scissors Rating System (✂ through ✂✂✂✂)

Each project in this book has a difficulty rating, noted just under the project title, that gives an idea of how difficult or time-consuming the bag is to make. The ratings are given in scissors—from one to four—with one being the easiest and four, the most complicated or difficult-to-sew projects. Obviously, these ratings are subjective. In general, though, a one-scissor rating means a project is quick and easy, appropriate for beginners (including children) or limited-time situations; and a four-scissors rating means the project requires experience and/or extra patience to complete. Keep in mind, *none* of these bags is terribly difficult (none, for instance, is as challenging as a tailored jacket); still, beginners and children should probably start with a one- or two-scissors rated project to ensure success.

Fabrics, Needles, and Threads

Most of the bags in this book can be made from "regular" fabric, readily available in fabric stores across the country; specific suggestions are given in the "You'll Need" box at the beginning of each project.

Sometimes, though, you'll want to select specialty fabrics; these include outdoor-type fabrics such as Cordura, and real or synthetic leathers, which are most readily available by mail order. While my first recommendation is to support local retailers, if you can't find it locally, mail-order vendors (at least those I have listed in the "Sources and Resources" section) are a reliable, helpful, and quick alternative source for these special fabrics.

Needles should be selected based on your fabric, as for any sewing project. Most of the bags I've made are of woven fabric, so I generally use sharps or universal points. For heavy fabrics, select a size 90/14 or 100/16. For light fabrics (such as linings and mesh), choose a fine needle, size 70/10 or 75/11. For all those average-weight fabrics, try an 80/12. And, of course, always start a new project with a new needle.

As for threads, remember two rules. First of all, buy the best-quality thread you can afford. It makes no sense to spend valuable time stitching a bag (or, for that matter, anything else) using a poor-quality thread; it will literally fall apart at the seams. So skip the bargain bins and head for the reputable brands (my personal favorites include Mettler, Coats, Mölnlycke, and Gütermann).

Second, select threads based on your fabric. The rule of thumb is to select a thread that is barely weaker than the fiber content of your fabric; that way, if anything rips, it'll be the thread (an easily repaired seam) rather than the fabric. When working with cotton, rayon, wool, or silk fabrics, I use cotton thread. If it's a substantial natural-fiber fabric, I use all-cotton quilting thread (Mettler has a nice one, in a wide variety of colors; try quilt shops if you're having trouble finding it). For the stronger polyester, nylon, and leather fabrics, I use 100% polyester thread. I rarely use nylon thread, even on nylon fabrics. Although it is the strongest thread of all, I find it difficult to work with, and it disintegrates with exposure to natural light and chlorine bleach.

Where to Look for Fabric and Supplies

For bags, generally, you'll want fabric that is more substantial than garment weight. Notions, too, will often need to be longer or heavier than those readily available in fabric stores. Fear not! Once you know where to look, you'll find what you need in the darndest places. For starters, check your yellow pages for:

"Fabric Shops": Traditional fabric stores will carry everything you need for many of the projects in this book. Look particularly in home-decorating (home-dec) departments for heavyweight fabrics (including tapestry, upholstery, and canvas for awnings and deck chairs), longer-length zippers, cording, and welting. Larger stores often carry a stiff plastic welting, which is a suitable choice for larger

bags like a zippered duffel. Look under this listing for independent stores that specialize in home-dec fabrics and supplies, too.

"Upholsterers," "Upholsterers' Supplies," and "Upholstery Fabrics": These retail stores and independent business folks often sell fabrics, hook-and-loop tape, twill tape, webbing, zippers, cording, welting, etc.

"Boat Covers, Tops & Upholstery," "Canvas Goods," and "Awnings & Canopies": Look for smaller shops or independent business folks who often sell fabrics, grommets (and grommet-setting services), webbing, plastic web-rings and snaphooks, toggles, zippers, etc.

"Camping Equipment" and "Mountain & Rock Climbing Equipment": Many of these stores will have a corner tucked away somewhere with a selection of webbings, plastic web-rings and snaphooks, toggles, zippers, fabrics, and such. If they don't have it on hand, they may be able to special order what you need.

"Leather": Look here for leather, of course, including leather handles and lacing . . . but also for findings like metal D- and O-rings, clasps, buckles, and snaps.

If you can't find what you need locally, turn to mail order. The "Sources and Resources" section at the end of this book lists those companies that I know about and what they specialize in. You may know of others. Check the classifieds in sewing magazines like *Threads* and *Sew News* for others.

I have found that most mail-order companies are very helpful. If you're not sure what you need, a customer service representative can usually help, or you can request samples (usually available for a small fee). The Green Pepper (see "Sources and Resources") does a particularly good job with samples, in my experience.

Mail-order companies' catalogs are often very informative, too. The Rain Shed (see "Sources and Resources"), for instance, has a great section in its catalog on using continuous zippers, among many other topics.

A Note on Sizes and Colors

Most of the webbing and plastic hardware (web-rings, snaphooks, sliders, and buckles) sold in fabric stores are available in the 1" size only. For other sizes (as well as for different weights of webbing), you'll probably have to find another type of supplier or use mail order.

Also, hardware colors are very limited, no matter where you shop. Most plastic hardware is available only in black; in metal, silver is most commonly available, followed by gold and then sometimes bronze. So, if you're making a bag with hardware, you might want to purchase the hardware first, then choose your fabric and notions to coordinate with it.

Techniques for Changing the Character of Your Fabric

If you just love a piece of fabric that is not substantial enough for a bag, you can often bolster garment-weight yardage to make it suitable. There are a number of techniques for doing this, including

Fusing: Fuse two layers of fabric together.

Layering: Stitch two layers of fabric together and treat as one.

Interfacing: Apply heavyweight or craft-weight interfacing.

Quilting: Quilt fabric to a layer of batting and lining (see Huge Quilted Duffel, Project #13, for machine-quilting tips).

Laminating: To create your own waterproof fabric, laminate 2-mil vinyl (available in fabric stores, usually in the home-dec department) using a low-temperature fusible web, such as HeatnBond Lite (see sidebar, page 36, for instructions).

A Note on Measurements

The projects in this book instruct you to purchase a certain amount of fabric and to cut it to specific measurements. Often, especially for "Flat Bags," these measurements are subjective.

For instance, a Camp Storage Bag can as easily be 11"×13" as the 12"×14" dictated by my instructions. So, if the cutter at the fabric store errs a bit on the short side or if you see a great remnant or if you happen already to have something on hand, don't panic if it's a bit shy of what's called for. Just use what you've got.

Of course, projects with lots of pieces that have to fit together just so (like the Quilter's Carryall) *do* require accurate measurement and cutting. Use your common sense.

1

Flat Bags

This first chapter covers the most basic of bag shapes, the flat square or rectangle that closes with either a zipper or a drawstring. These easiest-to-make bags are surprisingly versatile. By changing size, fabric, closures, and/or embellishments, flat bags can run the gamut from a utilitarian ditty bag to an elegant evening bag.

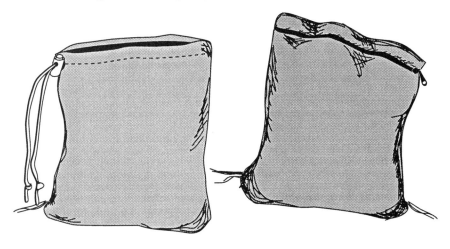

Project 1

Lightweight Carryall

| Difficulty: ✄ |

The ultimate lightweight carryall! This handy tote folds up on itself to fit into its own small front pocket—a mere 6"×8". When you need it, simply flip the pocket inside out to unfold a roomy 20"×22" bag with zippered top. Comfortable strap handles are the perfect length for carrying either over the shoulder or by hand. This is a great bag to pack when you travel, just in case you need a bit of extra storage on the return trip (perhaps for that perfect piece of fabric you bought, or for all the little goodies Grandma and Sis showered on the kids).

How to Make a Lightweight Carryall

1. Prepare fabric

a. Cut two 21½"×23" rectangles for front and back, plus one 7½"×16" rectangle for pocket, with long sides on the lengthwise grain. (*Note:* Do not include selvage in cuts.) *Optional:* Cut pocket from contrasting fabric.

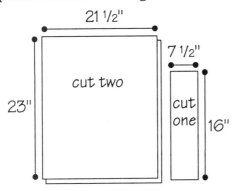

b.
Clean-finish top (21½") edge of front and back panels. *Optional:* Clean-finish all edges.

2. Apply pocket to front

a. Fold pocket panel in half crosswise, right sides together. Stitch ends together, using ½" seam allowance. Press seam open.

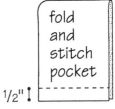

fold and stitch pocket

½"

b. Turn pocket right side out. Press flat, with seamline at bottom edge.

---

c. Mark centers at top edge of front panel and at top (folded) edge of pocket. (*Tip:* An easy way to mark centers is to fold in half and press lightly.)

d. Position pocket 1½" from top edge of front, aligning center marks. Pin. Edgestitch along sides and bottom.

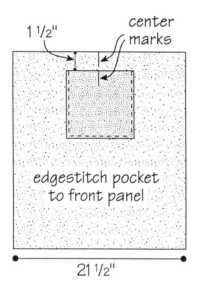

1 1/2"

center marks

edgestitch pocket to front panel

21 1/2"

3. Apply webbing

a. Mark webbing placement lines by extending the lines created by pocket sides to the top and bottom of front panel.

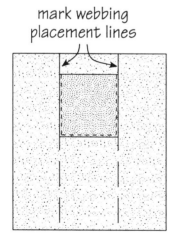

mark webbing placement lines

b. Mark identical placement lines on back panel. (*Tip:* Use chalk to mark the front, then place back panel on top, RST, and press together with your hand. The chalk marks will transfer to the back panel.)

c. Cut webbing into two 1¾-yard lengths.

d. Center one webbing strip over placement lines on front panel, beginning and ending at bottom edge, covering raw edges of pocket; webbing will loop over top of panel, forming handle. Pin. Edgestitch webbing into place, beginning at bottom of front panel and ending at top of pocket each time. Stitch, using a narrow zigzag, between edgestitching at pocket top, through pocket seam allowance.

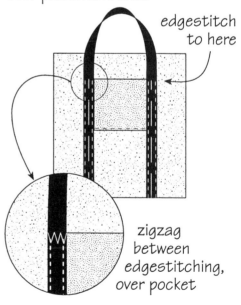

center webbing over placement lines

edgestitch to here

zigzag between edgestitching, over pocket

Hold It!

e. Repeat Step 3d for back panel, ending stitching 1½" from top edge (rather than at pocket top).

4. Insert zipper

a. Match top edge of front panel to one edge of zipper tape, right sides together. (*Tip:* If lengths don't match exactly, center fabric on zipper tape so equal lengths of fabric or tape extend at both ends.) Stitch about ⅛" from zipper teeth, taking care not to catch handle in seam.

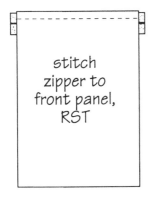

stitch zipper to front panel, RST

b. Stitch remaining side of zipper tape to back panel in the same manner as Step 4a.

c. Turn right side out. Edgestitch fabric to zipper tape along both sides.

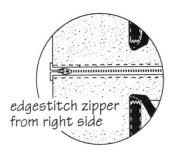

edgestitch zipper from right side

5. Finish bag

a. Unzip zipper about 5". Stitch or serge front to back panel, right sides together, along side and bottom edges, using ½" seam allowance. (*Note:* Adjust seam allowance if necessary to catch ends of zipper tape in seams.) Clean-finish edges.

Optional zipper tab(s): Before stitching side seams in Step 5a, place a short loop of webbing, ribbon, or tape (about a 3" length, folded in half) between two ends of zipper tape, just below teeth, on either or both sides; then stitch as in Step 5a, catching raw ends of loop in seam(s). This gives you something to grab when opening and closing zipper.

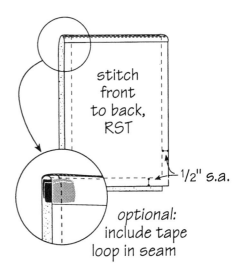

stitch front to back, RST

1/2" s.a.

optional: include tape loop in seam

b. Turn bag right side out. Square corners, using a turning tool if necessary.

6. Fold bag into pocket

a. Fold bag into thirds along webbing lines, folding sides toward back of bag.

fold sides toward back along webbing lines

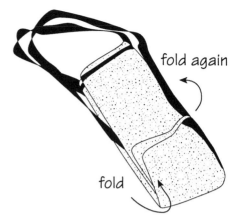

fold again

fold

b. Fold resulting strip into thirds, from bottom up, so entire bag is folded and layered behind pocket.

c. Hold all layers together firmly—except pocket—with one hand. With other hand, turn pocket inside out to enclose layers. Smooth.

Options, Ideas & Variations...

1 Insert a zipper in the flat pocket panel (before constructing and applying it in Step 2), to create a secure storage area between the two pocket layers. This is a handy spot to keep keys, change, or credit cards.

2 Make in a variety of sizes, with or without handles. A small bag without handles, stitched up in a quilted fabric, would make a nice jewelry or makeup tote.

3 Make a coordinating ditty bag (see Project #3) out of waterproof fabric, and take the duo to the beach, pool, or gym. A ⅜-yard length of a fabric such as Ultrex or Gore-Tex (at least 44" wide) is plenty to make both a stuff sack and a contrasting pocket.

Continuous-Zipper Construction Technique

This technique, borrowed from industry, makes sewing the Lightweight Carryall even faster and easier. It requires a length of zipper-by-the-yard, rather than a standard dress zipper (see the "Sources and Resources" section for mail-order sources). Personally, I like the medium-weight size 4.5 coil-type zipper for this bag, but the lightweight dress-size (2.5) and the slightly larger (and more widely available) size 5 also work fine, as do the corresponding tooth-type zippers I've tried.

The basic concept is to use just one half of the zipper tape (pull it apart down the middle), twice as long as the finished opening. Cut the bag in one piece (or stitch one side seam together so back and front are continuous). Stitch the zipper tape to the long edge in one piece. Then thread the zipper pull onto both ends of the tape; the bag will fold up on itself as it's zipped. The fold that forms at the other end when it's all zipped up becomes a very secure zipper stop.

To make the Lightweight Carryall using this technique:

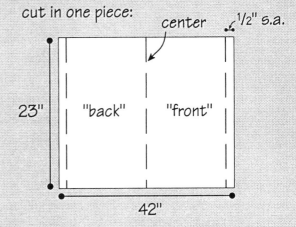

- Cut the fabric 23" x 42", rather than in two panels.

- Mark the center and the seam allowances (½") at each side. Designate one side the "front" and the other the "back."

- Follow the instructions up to the zipper step (Step 4), remembering to exclude the ½" seam allowance when finding the center front in Step 2c.

- In lieu of Step 4a, place zipper tape along top edge, right sides together, matching edges. Stitch about ⅛" from zipper teeth.

- In lieu of Step 4b, fold bag in half along center mark, wrong sides together. Thread zipper pull onto ends of zipper tape. Zip bag shut.

- Continue construction with Step 4c (you'll only have to stitch one side seam in Step 5a; the other's a fold).

Project 2

Camp Storage Bag

A place for everything, and everything in its place. While it's not too hard to know where "its place" is when you're at home, when you're out in the woods, on the road, or even at the beach, things have a way of getting rearranged every time you pack and unpack.

To keep things together, and—importantly—to be able to see at a glance what kind of things are in a particular bag, whip up a bunch of see-through storage bags in assorted sizes. What a great gift to keep your favorite traveler or camper happy!

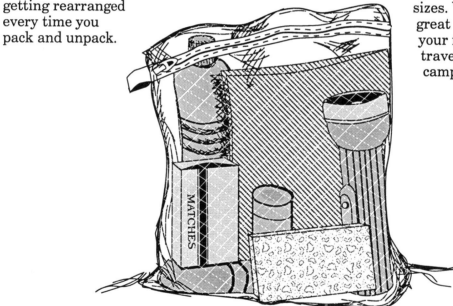

How to Make a Camp Storage Bag

You'll Need (for one 12"×14" bag)

Fabric: ½ yd. of a sturdy, see-through fabric, such as mesh or a drapery sheer, at least 36" wide

Notions: one 12" nylon dress zipper

Optional: 6" of ½"–1" twill tape or ribbon for zipper tab(s)

1. Prepare fabric

a. Cut a 13"×29" rectangle of fabric.

b. Clean-finish short (13") edges. *Optional:* Clean-finish all edges.

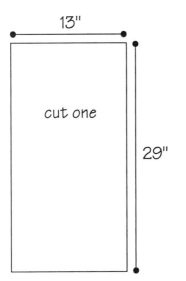

13"

cut one

29"

2. Insert zipper

a. Match one short edge of fabric to one edge of zipper tape, right sides together. (*Tip:* If lengths don't match exactly, center fabric on zipper tape so equal lengths of fabric or tape extend at both ends.) Stitch about ⅛" from zipper teeth.

stitch zipper to fabric, RST

b. Stitch remaining side of zipper tape to remaining short side of fabric in the same manner as Step 2a.

c. Turn right side out. Edgestitch fabric to zipper tape along both sides.

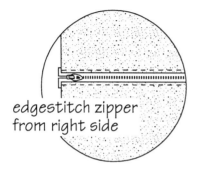

edgestitch zipper from right side

3. Finish bag

a. Open zipper about 5". Turn tube right sides together. Lay flat, with raw side edges aligned and zipper positioned flat at top (edge of zipper tape aligned with fold of fabric).

b. Stitch or serge sides, using ½" seam allowance. (*Note:* Adjust seam allowance if necessary to catch ends of zipper tape in seams.) *Optional:* Clean-finish edges.

Optional: Before stitching side seams in Step 3b, place a short loop of twill tape or ribbon (about a 3" length, folded in half) between fabric layers on either or both sides, centered on zipper teeth, matching raw edges; then stitch,

catching raw ends of loop in seam(s). This gives you something to grab when opening and closing the zipper.

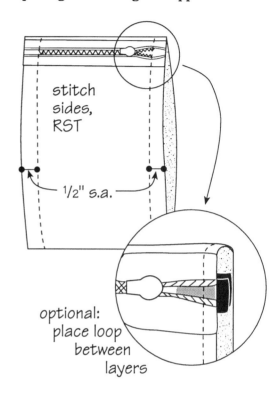

stitch sides, RST

½" s.a.

optional: place loop between layers

c. Turn bag right side out. Square corners, using a turning tool if necessary.

d. *Optional:* Edgestitch sides from top to just past zipper tape, to keep bag flat at top sides and to reinforce tabs.

Options, Ideas & Variations...

1 Make Camp Storage Bags in different sizes for different items. To figure cutting measurements, use this formula:

- First, determine the finished size (e.g., 15"×10").
- To these measurements, multiply the length by two (e.g., 15" × 2 = 30").
- Then add 1" to this new length (e.g., 30" + 1" = 31") and also to the width measurement (e.g., 10" + 1" = 11").
- So, for a finished bag that is 15"×10", cut the fabric 31"×11".

2 Move the zipper. For example, make a large mesh bag with the zipper positioned midway between the top and bottom, to hang over a clothesline or branch. Use it to keep supplies out of reach of wildlife or to hang small objects out to dry.

3 Give a bag filled with first-aid supplies to your favorite Scout troop or camper.

Among the items you might want to include are

- adhesive bandages, steri-pads, gauze, and adhesive tape
- disinfectant soap (e.g., Dial) and a washcloth
- tweezers, needle, and matches
- instant ice pack
- rubber gloves and a Ziploc bag
- cravats (large triangular bandages, 45"×45" on the sides) safety pins, and splints
- change for a pay phone
- first-aid book

4 Make pretty see-through bags out of lace to keep hosiery and lingerie run-free during travel, or make several out of a soft net fabric for carefree laundering of your fine washables.

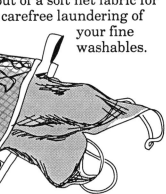

Project 3

Travel Laundry Bag

Difficulty: ✂

This is the ubiquitous "ditty bag" so familiar to sailors and Scouts. Legend has it the name comes from the *dittus* or Manchester cloth from which they were once made, although today nothing is known of such a fabric.

Nevertheless, these all-purpose double-drawstring bags still come in handy for a multitude of uses, ranging from lacy potpourri bags to sleeping-bag stuff sacks. A small bag made out of

quilted decorator chintz makes a perfect makeup or jewelry bag. Or how about one out of waterproof fabric for wet towels and suits, and another made out of mesh to hold sandy beach toys? The directions that follow are for making an all-purpose bag—the perfect size to pack for travel, to keep dirty clothes separate from the clean ones till a washing machine turns up. (Where do *you* put your dirty clothes when you travel?)

How to Make a Travel Laundry Bag

You'll Need (for one 21"×25" bag)

Fabric: ⅝ yd. of a lightweight, tightly woven fabric such as nylon Supplex, ripstop, or taffeta, about 54" wide (or ¾ yd. of 45"-wide fabric)

Notions: 3¼ yd. of ⅛" flat or round cording, cut in half

bodkin (or a safety pin)

1. Prepare fabric

a. Cut two 26"×22" panels of fabric.

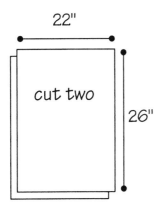

22"

cut two

26"

b. Clean-finish side edges.

2. Stitch side seams

Place panels right sides together, matching edges. Stitch side seams, using ½" seam allowance and leaving a ⅜" opening in stitching line 1⅛" from top edge on both sides (for drawstrings). Stitch or serge bottom seam, using ½" seam allowance; clean-finish edge if not serged. Finger-press side seams open near top.

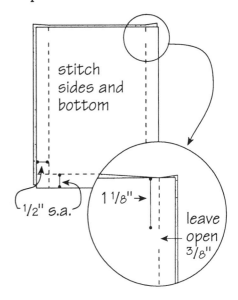

stitch sides and bottom

½" s.a.

1 ⅛"→

leave open ⅜"

3. Create casing

Fold and press under ⅜" along top edge. Fold and press under again, this time ⅝" along top edge. Edgestitch along first fold.

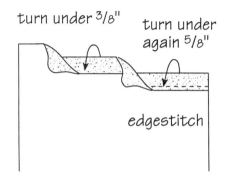

turn under ³/₈" turn under again ⁵/₈"

edgestitch

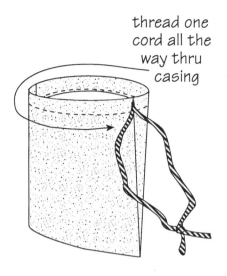

thread one cord all the way thru casing

4. Finish bag

a. Turn bag right side out.

b. Thread one piece of cording through entire casing, beginning and ending at same side-seam opening. Knot ends.

c. Thread remaining piece of cording through entire casing, beginning and ending at opposite side-seam opening. Knot ends.

d. Draw bag shut by pulling cords in opposite directions.

Options, Ideas & Variations...

1 Stitch a large net or mesh bag for transporting kids' (sandy) beach toys. (*Tip:* Bind the edges with lace seam binding for easiest stitching on large mesh.)

2 Make a waterproof (Gore-Tex or Ultrex) bag for the beach or pool.

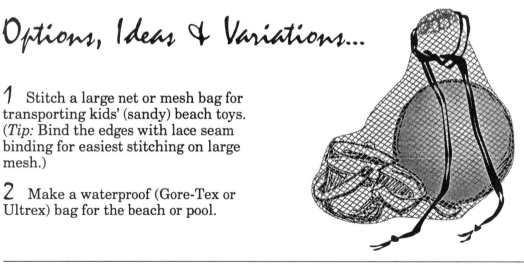

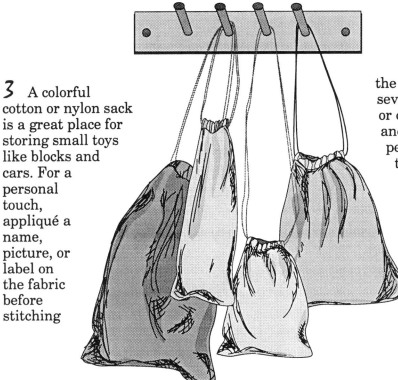

3 A colorful cotton or nylon sack is a great place for storing small toys like blocks and cars. For a personal touch, appliqué a name, picture, or label on the fabric before stitching the bag together. Make several in coordinating or contrasting colors, and hang from hooks or pegs. Not only are the toys easily accessible, but the bags add an attractive decorative accent to your favorite person's play area.

4 Consider making a small version for holding golf balls and tees, maybe with a grosgrain ribbon stitched across the front in loops to keep a couple of tees within easy grasping range.

5 A slippery nylon stuff sack makes pillow and sleeping bag storage neat and easy.

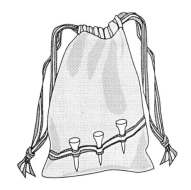

---

*Chapter 1: **Flat Bags***

Project 4

Shoe Travel Bags

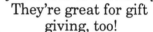

Difficulty:

The next time you travel, protect your clean clothes from dirty soles with these quick-and-easy-to-make shoe bags. The mesh panel lets you see at a glance what's

inside, and also keeps your shoes well aired. Make several pairs in different sizes for every member of the family. They're great for gift giving, too!

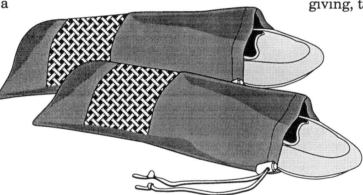

How to Make Shoe Travel Bags

You'll Need (for one pair of Shoe Travel Bags)

Fabric: ⅜ yd. for adult sizes, or ¼ yd. for youth/child sizes, of a soft, tightly woven fabric such as cotton chamois or flannel, at least 60" wide (when using 44"-wide fabric, double the yardage for all but child's size)

⅛ yd. of medium- to heavyweight mesh, such as fishnet (white for easiest see-through)

Notions: 1¾ yd. of ⅛" cording, cut in half, or one pair of 28" or longer shoelaces

bodkin (or a safety pin)

Optional: one pair toggles

1. Prepare fabrics

a. Cut two rectangles of fabric and two of mesh for each pair of bags, as follows:

Size	Fabric	Mesh
Man's	9"×30"	4"×9"
Woman's	8"×28"	4"×8"
Youth's	7"×26"	3"×7"
Child's	6"×22"	3"×6"

cut two of fabric

cut two of mesh

b. Cut each fabric panel crosswise into two sections:

- 18½" from end for man's
- 17½" from end for woman's
- 15½" from end for youth's
- 13½" from end for child's

cut each into two sections

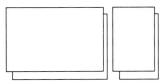

c. *Optional:* Clean-finish all edges.

2. Insert mesh

a. Stitch or serge mesh strips between fabric sections, using ½" seam allowance. *Optional:* Clean-finish edges of seam allowances.

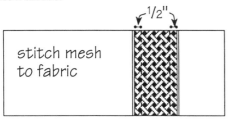

b. Finger-press seams toward fabric. Topstitch.

3. Stitch side seams

a. Clean-finish edges on both short ends of both panels (if you didn't already clean-finish edges in Step 1c).

b. Fold each panel in half crosswise, right sides together. Stitch side seams using ½" seam allowance, leaving a ½"

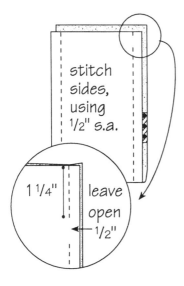

opening 1¼" from top edge of one side seam (for drawstrings).

b. Finger-press seams open for about 3" from top edge.

4. Create casing

a. Turn bags right side out.

b. Fold top edge of one bag 1" to inside to form casing; press. Stitch ⅞" from edge of fabric, through all layers. Repeat for remaining bag.

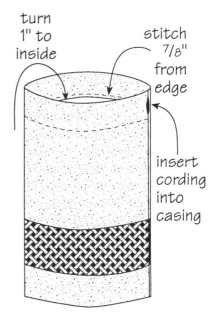

5. Finish bags

a. Insert one cord into casing through hole in side seam of one bag. Knot each end; tie to close bag. Repeat for remaining bag. Press bags flat if desired.

b. *Optional:* Thread cord ends through a toggle for each bag, before knotting in Step 5a; slide toggles up to close bags.

Project 5

Garment Storage Bag

Difficulty: ✂

Keep dust and dirt off your clothes during the off-season with this Garment Storage Bag. Each bag holds eight to ten garments, to give you lots of versatility. The full-length zipper is placed in the side seam, to make it easy to get things in and out. Make it out of unbleached muslin for strictly practical storage, or pick a pretty print to coordinate with your decorating scheme. These bags are simple, fast, and inexpensive to make—and oh so useful. What a practical gift, too.

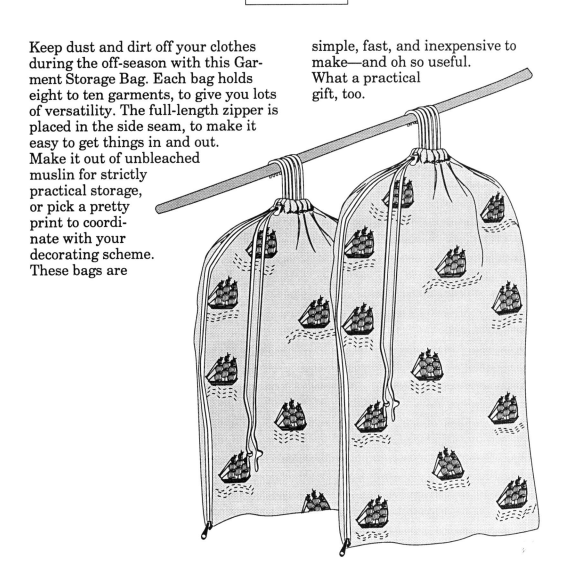

How to Make a Garment Storage Bag

You'll Need (for one 39"×35" [short] or one 59"×39" [long] bag)

Fabric: 2¼ yd. for short bag (36"-wide fabric) or 3⅜ yd. for long bag (44"-wide fabric)

scrap of fabric, about 3½"×1"

Notions: 1 yd. of ⅛" to ¼" flat or round cording

2¼ yd. for short bag or 3⅜ yd. for long bag of size 2.5 or dress-weight zipper-by-the-yard (you'll only use one side) and one zipper pull

one toggle

bodkin (or a safety pin)

1. Prepare fabric

Trim fabric to about
- 36" wide for short bag
- 40" wide for long bag

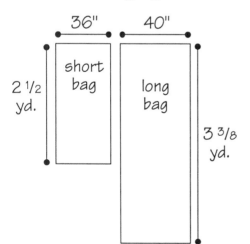

2. Insert zipper

a. Place zipper on one long edge of fabric, right sides together, matching edges. Stitch close to zipper teeth, beginning and ending stitching 3½" from ends of fabric.

3 ½"

stitch zipper to fabric, RST

b. Fold fabric in half crosswise, wrong sides together. Thread zipper pull onto zipper tape; zip closed. (*Note: Zipper pull will be at bottom of bag when closed.*)

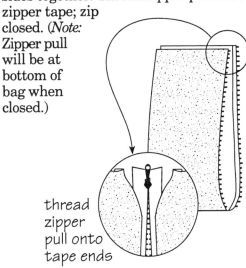

thread zipper pull onto tape ends

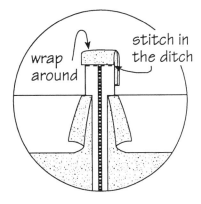

wrap around

stitch in the ditch

f. Finish stitching bag fabric to zipper tape, to end of stop.

3. Stitch side seam

Turn bag right sides together. Stitch or serge remaining side seam, using a ½" seam allowance. Turn right side out.

c. Trim ends of zipper tape even, 2¼" from ends of fabric.

d. Mark center of an approximately 3½"×1" scrap of fabric. Fold bag fabric down, out of the way of zipper ends. Align mark ½" from zipper ends, right sides together. Stitch scrap to zipper tape along mark.

4. Create casing for drawstring

a. Serge off or turn under ½" at top edge. Fold down 1¼" to inside to form casing; press. Stitch 1" from edge of fabric, through all layers.

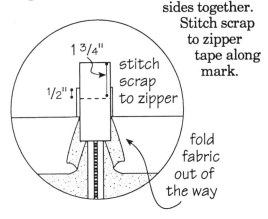

1 3/4"

stitch scrap to zipper

1/2"

fold fabric out of the way

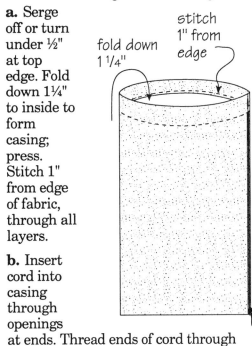

stitch 1" from edge

fold down 1 1/4"

b. Insert cord into casing through openings at ends. Thread ends of cord through toggle; pull to gather shut.

e. Wrap scrap over and around raw ends of zipper tape to finish edge and create a stop. Stitch in the ditch.

Project 6

Jingle-Bell Gift Bag

Difficulty: ✂

This easy and festive gift wrap for a bottle of holiday cheer features a pretty contrasting facing and a dozen jingle bells chiming a seasonal tune. Use it for other gifts, too . . . maybe a can of tennis balls, a stack of Play-Doh, or anything else tall and skinny. Change the color scheme and substitute charms or beads for the bells, and you've got a unique wrap for any holiday or special occasion. Plus, it's a great project for using up leftover fabric.

How to Make a Jingle-Bell Gift Bag

1. Prepare fabric

Piece fabric if desired. Cut one 13"×17" rectangle of main fabric. Cut one 13"×5" rectangle of facing fabric.

2. Apply facing

a. Clean-finish one 13" edge of facing. (*Tip:* Serge a thin strip of fusible web to wrong side while clean-finishing edge, or serge with fusible thread in the lower looper, for easiest basting in Step 2c.)

b. Match raw 13" edge of facing to one 13" edge of fabric, right sides together. Stitch or serge, using a ¼" seam allowance. Press seam open. (*Note:* Be

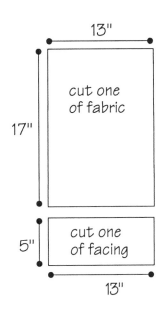

careful not to touch iron to fusible web or thread, if you used it in Step 2a.)

stitch RST

↕ ¼" s.a.

← clean-
finish
edge

c. Turn fabrics along seamline, wrong sides together. Press flat. Baste lower edge of facing to fabric.

3. Apply ribbons

a. Mark ribbon placement line 4½" down from top edge (or use stitching line if you stitch-basted the facing).

b. Cut ¼" ribbon into 13 pieces: one 27", two 10", two 9", two 8", two 7", two 6", and two 5". Set the 27" piece aside.

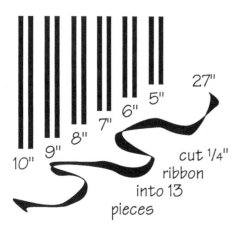

27"

5"

6"

7"

8"

9"

10"

cut ¼"
ribbon
into 13
pieces

c. Arrange 12 short pieces of ribbon to hang perpendicular to placement line, beginning and ending 1" from side edges of fabric and spacing ribbons approximately evenly. Glue-baste (use a small dot of white fabric glue) the tip of each ribbon to fabric on placement mark.

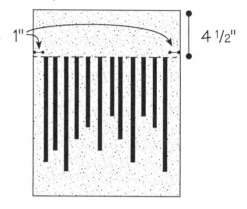

glue-baste ribbons
to placement line

1"

4 ½"

4. Create casing

Press under ½" on each end of ½" (or ⅝") ribbon. Center over ribbon placement line, covering ends of glue-basted ribbon pieces. Pin. Edgestitch both long sides, leaving ends open.

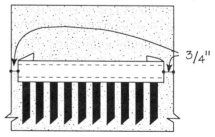

center ½" ribbon over placement
line; edgestitch long sides only

¾"

5. Finish bag

a. Fold fabric right sides together, keeping ribbons out of the way. Stitch or serge side and bottom seams, using ½" seam allowance.

Optional: Trim seam allowances to ¼"; clean-finish. Tack seam allowance to one side at top edge.

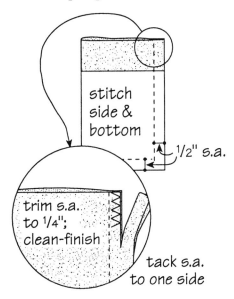

stitch side & bottom

½" s.a.

trim s.a. to ¼"; clean-finish

tack s.a. to one side

b. Turn bag right side out. Thread 27" piece of ¼" ribbon through casing. (*Tip:* A large-eyed, blunt-tipped tapestry needle works well for this.)

c. Tie jingle bells to ends of 12 hanging pieces of ribbon.

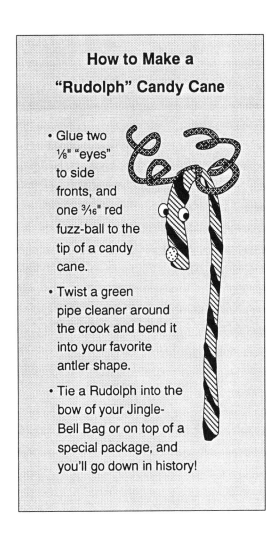

How to Make a "Rudolph" Candy Cane

- Glue two ⅛" "eyes" to side fronts, and one ³⁄₁₆" red fuzz-ball to the tip of a candy cane.

- Twist a green pipe cleaner around the crook and bend it into your favorite antler shape.

- Tie a Rudolph into the bow of your Jingle-Bell Bag or on top of a special package, and you'll go down in history!

Project 7

Evening "Crazy" Belt Bag

Difficulty: ✐✐✐

In the last quarter of the nineteenth century in the United States, crazy quilts—also known at the time as "puzzle patchwork" or "Japanese patchwork"—were all the rage; yet, by 1920, they had all but disappeared.

The 1876 Centennial Exhibition held in Philadelphia is generally regarded as the design inspiration for this fad in American quilting. The Japanese Pavilion there was the most popular exhibit at the fair, exposing 9.5 million visitors to the exotic fabrics and design motifs of this Far Eastern culture. The luxurious silk, velvet, and brocade scraps that were the hallmark of crazy quilts were often traded among friends and relatives or purchased by mail from textile factories. By 1885, ready-to-sew crazy quilt kits even were being advertised!

Crazy quilts were generally small, made for display rather than use; crazy quilting was a symbol of upper-class freedom, giving tangible evidence that the woman of the house was sufficiently well provided for that she could spend time on such domestic niceties as stitching purely decorative items, while servants took care of the household chores.

This small project is a great introduction to contemporary crazy quilting. It's the perfect little bag for carrying an evening's essentials. Make it from fabric to match or coordinate with your outfit, and wear it draped over a belt for an interesting and functional accessory. Further the decorative effect by hanging coins, beads, or other findings from the cords. Or make it in a larger size for a unique and elegant evening handbag. Round out the bottom for added dimension by pinching the corners together and tacking them at center with a custom-made tassel.

How to Make an Evening "Crazy" Belt Bag

1. Prepare fabric

a. Cut one 13"×11" lining.

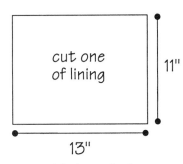

cut one of lining — 11" — 13"

b. Crazy-piece fabric and trims to make a 13"×10½" rectangle. (*Note:* See box, next page, for three methods of crazy-piecing; use whichever one is most comfortable for you.)

Tip: You might begin by sketching possible designs on paper. Be sure to consider where the front, back, casing, seam, and fold will fall when designing your pieced fabric. Their positions are shown below:

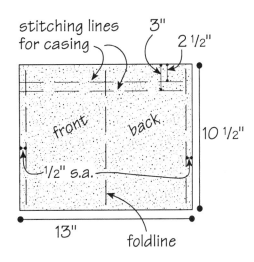

stitching lines for casing — 3" — 2½" — front — back — 10½" — ½" s.a. — 13" — foldline

How to Crazy-Piece Fabrics

Three of the most popular ways to join fabrics when crazy-piecing are

- seam the raw edges, right sides together

- lap raw edges, and cover with trim

- fold under one raw edge, lap, and stitch (insert trim before stitching, if desired)

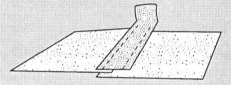

It's not necessary, but you may build your crazy patchwork on a foundation cut slightly larger than the finished size. Lightweight muslin, tear-away stabilizer, and paper are all suitable choices for a foundation. Trim to size after piecing.

c. Once the fabrics are joined, embellish the seamlines by stitching over them, either by hand or by machine, using fancy decorative stitches and colorful embroidery threads.

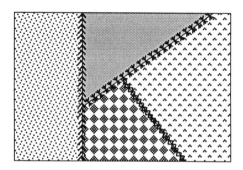

d. *Optional:* Clean-finish edges on pieced panel and lining.

2. Stitch side seams

a. Fold pieced panel, right sides together, matching 10½" edges. Stitch, using ½" seam allowance, leaving ½" open 2½" from top edge of fabric.

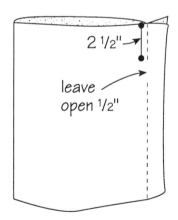

2 ½" →

leave open ½"

b. Fold lining panel in half, right sides together, matching 11" edges. Stitch or serge, using ½" seam allowance.

3. Stitch lining to fabric

a. Turn lining right side out. Slip inside tube of pieced fabric (they'll be right sides together), matching side seams and raw top edges. Stitch around top edge, using ¼" seam allowance.

b. Turn right sides out, so lining wraps snugly over seam allowance at top. Pin in place.

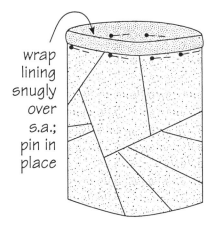

wrap
lining
snugly
over
s.a.;
pin in
place

4. Create casing

a. Measure 2½" from top edge; mark

with pins. Measure and mark again 3" from top edge.

b. Stitch along marked lines, making sure opening along seamline falls between them.

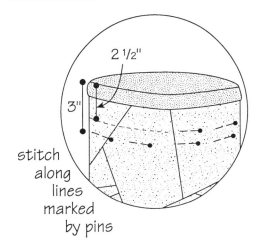

2 ½"

3"

stitch
along
lines
marked
by pins

5. Finish bag

a. Turn inside out. Stitch or serge across bottom raw edges, through all layers, using ½" seam allowance. If not serged, trim to ¼" and clean-finish.

b. Turn right side out. Thread cord through casing. Add coins or beads to ends, if desired, or knot ends together.

Evening "Crazy" Handbag Variation...

a. Cut fabric (pieced or whole cloth) 16"×14"; cut lining 16"×14½".

b. Construct as for belt bag, through Step 5a. Turn right side out.

c. Round out bottom by tacking corners to center of bottom seam. To tack, pinch a fold in bottom seam at center, perpendicular to seamline. Fold each corner up to meet on opposite sides of pinched center fold, matching seamlines. Tack through all layers.

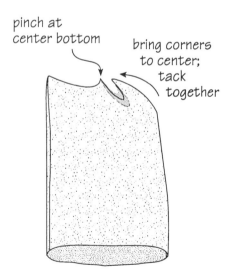

pinch at center bottom

bring corners to center; tack together

d. Make matching cording and tassel. (You'll need about 18 yards of heavy decorative thread, such as Candlelight metallic or Pearl Crown Rayon, and about 3 yards of rattail cord.)

To make cording: Loosely braid one strand of rattail cord and two strands of thread, each 1½ yards long. Knot ends.

To make tassel: Cut and lightly tape (at both ends) a 6" length of thread across a 4"×6" piece of cardboard. Wrap remaining thread around the cardboard about 30 times, perpendicular to taped piece of thread; do not cut. Wrap remaining 1½ yards of rattail cord over the thread. Continue wrapping thread over rattail, another 30 to 40 times. Untape the 6" thread, and slide it to one edge of cardboard; tie tightly and securely. Clip through threads and cord at opposite edge to release strands from cardboard. Wrap with decorative thread about ¾" down from knot to finish tassel.

e. Stitch tassel to center bottom. Thread cording through casing; tie ends together.

2

Totes

Totes are defined as "large and capacious bags" according to *The New Little Oxford Dictionary* (Oxford University Press, 1990)—a description that covers a lot of territory! For the purposes of this chapter, tote bags are flat bags at heart . . . but ones that have been given shape by stitching across the two lower corners, thereby forming a rectangular bottom and sides. Even so, there are many variations, as you will see.

Classic Open Tote

The open tote is an enduring style, both easy to make and well suited to a wide variety of uses. This is the "free tote bag" that all manner of merchandisers offer as a premium to induce you to buy their wares; the "boat bag" that sporting goods companies like L.L. Bean have been selling for years; the upscale "museum bag" that our finest cultural institutions offer through gift shops and catalogs, many of them with a hefty price tag attached; and the "ecological grocery bag" that will help save our planet from the evils of paper and plastic sacks. Your fabric choice—which may range from plain, unbleached canvas to upholstery fabrics, leathers, tapestries, and even wools—will determine whether you'll end up with a designer original or a utilitarian carryall. The following instructions are for making a plain, slightly oversize "green" grocery bag, but it's easy to change the size and look to suit your every need.

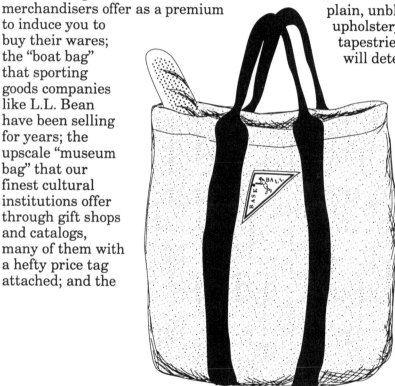

How to Make a Classic Open Tote

You'll Need *(for one 18"×13"×7" bag)*

Fabric: 1³⁄₈ yd. sturdy fabric, such as canvas, denim, Cordura, or pack cloth, at least 44" wide (*Note:* This is enough fabric for two bags.)

Optional: contrasting fabric for bottom (see Option 2, page 35, for measurements)

Notions: 3¼ yd. of 1½" webbing

chalk or other marker; ruler

Optional: decorative patch, label, or appliqué

1. Prepare fabric

Cut fabric to 22"×48", with length on the lengthwise grain.

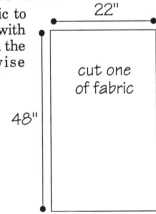

22"

48"

cut one of fabric

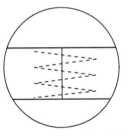

b. Quarter-mark webbing, using butt joint as one of the four marks.

c. Measure and mark 6" to either side of two opposite quarter marks (this will define two 12" segments, the handles).

2. Prepare webbing

a. Clean-finish ends of webbing: sear nylon and polypropylene; stitch or fold under cotton and blends. Butt ends together snugly; stitch back and forth several times to secure. (*Note:* Be sure webbing isn't twisted before stitching.)

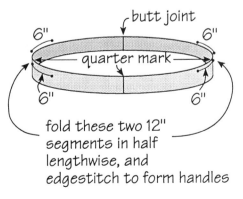

butt joint

6"   6"

quarter mark

6"   6"

fold these two 12" segments in half lengthwise, and edgestitch to form handles

d. Fold webbing in half lengthwise along each 12" segment. Edgestitch to form handles.

3. Apply webbing

a. Mark center bottom line midway across width of fabric. Mark webbing placement lines on right side, 8½" in from each long edge.

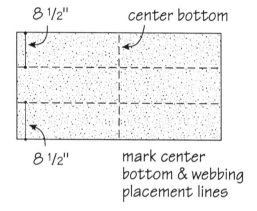

8 ½"   center bottom

8 ½"   mark center
bottom & webbing
placement lines

b. Position webbing on right side of fabric, inside edges along placement lines, positioning butt joint and remaining quarter mark on center bottom line; handles will loop over ends of panel. Pin.

c. Edgestitch webbing, beginning and ending about 5" from each edge of panel.

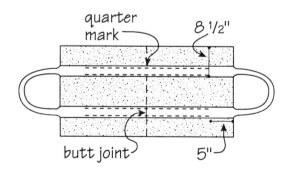

quarter
mark   8 ½"

butt joint   5"

4. Stitch side seams and hem

a. Fold panel right sides together along center bottom line. Stitch or serge side seams, using ½" seam allowance. *Optional:* Trim seam allowance to ¼" and clean-finish if not serged.

b. Fold top raw edge under 1"; finger-press. Fold under again 1"; finger-press. Edgestitch.

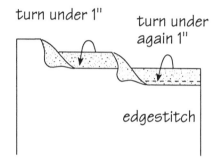

turn under 1"   turn under
again 1"

edgestitch

5. Create bottom

a. Flatten one corner to create a triangular point, aligning side seam with center bottom line.

b. Mark a 7"-long line perpendicular to seam, 3½" from point. Stitch along line. Stitch again ⅛" from seam, toward point, to reinforce. Repeat for other corner.

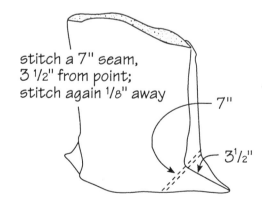

stitch a 7" seam,
3 ½" from point;
stitch again ⅛" away

7"

3½"

6. Finish bag

Finish stitching webbing to bag at top, to within ¾" of edge. Reinforce between stitching lines, using a narrow zigzag.

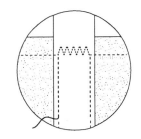

Options, Ideas & Variations...

1 Make a Classic Open Tote in any size. To determine cutting dimensions, use this formula:

- Length will be finished height times two, plus finished depth, plus 2"–5" (2" for smaller bags, up to 5" for larger bags).

- Width will be finished width, plus finished depth, plus 1"–2" (1" for smaller bags, up to 2" for larger bags).

- Webbing will be finished height times four, plus finished depth times two, plus finished handle length times two (handle length generally ranges from 10" each for teeny totes to 16" each for grocery-bag–size totes).

2 Add a contrasting bottom. This is a practical as well as decorative option; the extra layer reinforces the bottom, which has to stand up to the most wear. To add this option, you'll need a piece of contrasting fabric the same width as the bag fabric, but 3"–7" longer than the bag's depth (3" for small bags, up to 7" for large bags).

a. Construct as for Classic Open Tote, through Step 3c.

b. Press under ½" on each long side of contrast panel.

c. Edgestitch panel to bag at center bottom, right sides up.

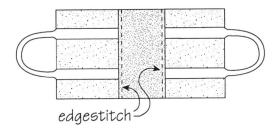

edgestitch

d. Complete Step 4.

e. Turn bag right side out. Stitch corners as in Step 5a, except working on right side of bag. Fold triangular points up along each side, matching seamlines; pin. Stitch in the ditch through all layers to secure corners to bag.

3 Attach a gripper snap at center front to hold the bag closed.

4 For a crisper look, edgestitch all four sides, from top edge to bottom corners.

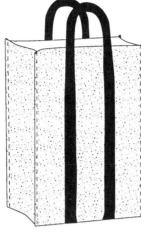

5 If you don't need the strength of wrap-around webbing, use shorter handles. Either stitch them behind the hem at top, or anchor them to the outside with decorative swatches of fabric, such as leather or Ultrasuede.

6 If it's important that the bag be waterproof, choose a laminated fabric for your tote. Purchase already-laminated yardage, or laminate it yourself (see sidebar for instructions).

How to Laminate Fabric

To laminate your own fabric, you'll need equal yardages of fabric, fusible web, and clear vinyl. Choose one of the new low-temperature fusible webs, such as HeatnBond Lite, and a thin (such as 2-mil) vinyl; both are readily available in fabric stores (try the home-dec department for vinyl).

- Fuse the web to the right side of your fabric, following the manufacturer's directions.

- Place clear vinyl on top of the fusible web, taking care to smooth out any wrinkles.

- Place the tissue paper that comes with the vinyl on top of the vinyl-web-fabric sandwich. Press on top of the paper, using approximately a silk/wool setting, until vinyl is fused securely to fabric. (*Tip:* Test to determine the proper heat setting: too hot, and you will melt the vinyl; too cool, and it will not adhere.)

- After fusing, stitch or serge around all the edges to keep the layers securely together.

Alternatively, purchase Fab-Lam (see "Sources and Resources"), which is a one-step iron-on laminate, or Converseal (available in art-supply stores), which is self-adhesive (no heat required). *Whatever your choice, remember to test first.*

Hold It!

Plate 1

Clockwise from top:
Toy Storage Set (p. 15)
Expandable Zippered Tote (p. 42)
Travel Organizer, in Cordura (p. 88)
Insulated Lunch Bag (p. 38)
Golf-Tee Bag (p. 15)
　　Laminated Classic Open Tote (p. 36)
　　　Lightweight Carryall, shown open and
　　　　folded (p. 2)

Plate 2

From top to bottom:

Leather String Duffel (p. 54)

Expandable Zippered Tote, shown expanded and closed (p. 42)

Donn's Tool Roll, shown rolled and open (p. 100)

Gardener's Tote (p. 37)

Plate 4

Clockwise from top:
Mesh Beach-Bag (p. 14)
Super Sports Bag, in Cordura (p. 70)
Reversible Child's Play Mat, shown open and
   closed (p. 96)

7 Add a pocket. Stitch a small one either inside or outside, between the webbing; use hook-and-loop tape as a closure, to keep coupons, checks, pen, credit cards, keys, cash, etc. securely inside. Or perhaps you need a large inside pocket, channel-stitched vertically every inch, to keep knitting needles in place.

8 Pamper yourself or a favorite green-thumbed friend with a handy garden tote. Toss in a new pair of gloves, a trowel, and some seeds or bulbs to complete the ensemble (for a 10" h, 13" w, 5" d finished bag, cut fabric to 30" × 20").

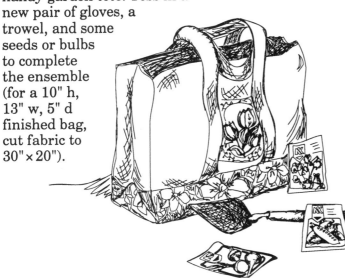

9 Stitch an appliqué or decorative patch or label to the front, or satin-stitch a monogram to personalize your bag.

10 Stencil, paint, or appliqué the bag for a unique creation.

11 Teeny totes are great for kids, and also for holding special hostess gifts . . . like a pair of mugs with mulled cider spices tucked in . . . or maybe a mason jar filled with layers of colorful dried beans and your favorite hearty soup recipe (for a 6" h, 5" w, 4" d finished bag, cut fabric to 19" × 10").

Project 9

Insulated Lunch Bag

Difficulty: ✄✄

Fabric lunch bags are the save-a-tree alternative to paper sacks. And this one has the added advantages of being insulated, washable, and attractive. No more mix-ups in the school cafeteria either; there'll be no mistaking this unique bag for run-of-the-mill issue. Make one for each member of the family in his or her favorite color. Also, consider making it in a larger size and adding backpack-style straps; what a practical way to carry the entire family's lunch to your next picnic outing.

How to Make an Insulated Lunch Bag

You'll Need (for one 15" × 8" × 4" bag)

Fabric: ⅜ yd. each: light- to medium-weight outer fabric; coordinating lining fabric; and thin insulating fabric, such as Thinsulate or Warm Winter (all fabrics at least 36" wide and washable; consider a waterproof or water-resistant fabric such as nylon Supplex for the lining, to protect against leakage and spills)

Notions: 1¾ yd. of ¾" webbing

one ¾" side-release buckle (also called a parachute clip)

one ¾" tabler buckle (also called a ladder buckle)

(*Note:* Small fingers may prefer a larger buckle; 1" webbing and hardware may be substituted for ¾".)

1. Prepare fabric

Cut outer fabric to 13" × 36"; cut insulating fabric to 13" × 35¾"; cut lining to 13" × 35¼".

36" for fabric
35 3/4" for insulating fabric
35 1/4" for lining

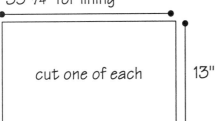

cut one of each   13"

2. Stitch layers together

a. Stack layers as follows: insulating fabric, right side up; fabric, right side up; lining, wrong side up. Stitch both short ends, using ½" seam allowance.

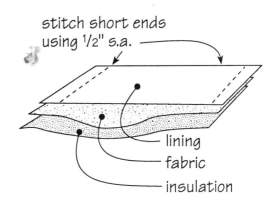

stitch short ends using 1/2" s.a.

lining
fabric
insulation

Note: Don't worry that the layers won't lay flat; just match the raw edges.

b. Place hand between lining and fabric layers. Shift fabric so lining is on one side, fabric and insulation on the other, with seams in the middle. Pin raw edges together, matching seams.

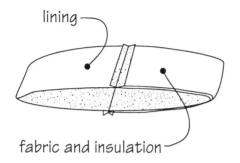

c. Stitch both sides, using ½" seam allowances and leaving a 5" opening 3" from fold of lining on one side. (*Tip:* Stretch insulation slightly to stitch without creating tucks in fabric.) Press seam allowances open.

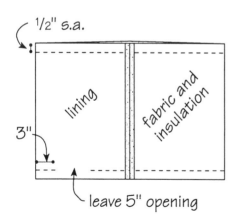

d. Turn right side out through opening. Stitch opening closed. (*Note:* Slipstitch by hand if you're a perfectionist, or edgestitch by machine if you're a pragmatist.)

3. Create bottom

a. Stuff fabric/insulation into lining to create bag shape (it'll be wrong side out).

b. Flatten one corner to create a triangular point, aligning side seam with center bottom. Mark a 4"-long line perpendicular to seam, 2" from point. Stitch or serge along line. Repeat for other corner.

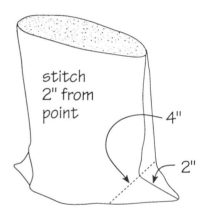

c. *Optional:* If not serged, trim corner seam allowances to ½" and clean-finish.

d. Turn bag right side out.

4. Attach webbing and hardware

a. Cut webbing into three pieces: 4", 8", and 50". Clean-finish ends (sear nylon and polypropylene; zigzag cotton).

b. Loop 4" piece through side-release buckle. Stitch to top edge of bag at center, with buckle hanging just over edge (stitch in a rectangle for most secure attachment).

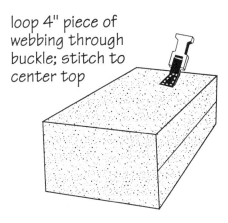

loop 4" piece of webbing through buckle; stitch to center top

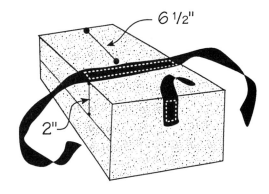

6 ½"

2"

c. Turn bag over. Stitch center of 50" piece of webbing crosswise to bag, 6½" down from top, beginning and ending 2¼" from each side seam. Stitch end of 8" piece to center of bottom edge, as shown in drawing. (Again, stitch in a rectangle for most secure attachment.)

d. Thread tongue piece of side-release buckle onto 8" webbing.

e. Thread one end of 50" webbing through smooth end of tabler buckle. Stitch close to buckle to secure. Thread remaining end of webbing up and back through tabbed end of buckle.

5. Finish bag

Push sides in to form 2" pleats above shoulder strap. Fold bag over webbing at center; clip side-release buckle shut.

Project 10

Expandable Zippered Tote

Difficulty: ✂✂

This fully lined tote bag is versatile
and roomy and sports a fold-out
extension at the top that lets you add
5" to the height of the bag whenever
you need it. Whether it's tucked in or
folded out, the extension zips shut to
keep your contents safe and
secure. For shopping, beach,
picnic, or playground, consider
adding a hidden zippered
pocket on the underside of the
extension to hold keys, cash,
coupons, etc. Or whip up some
simple accessories such as a
changing pad, an insulated
bottle bag, a waterproof diaper
bag, and a couple of burping
towels—a great gift for your
favorite new mom and dad.

If you're one who prefers to
shoulder your load rather than to
tote it, you'll want to include the
optional shoulder strap for even
greater versatility.

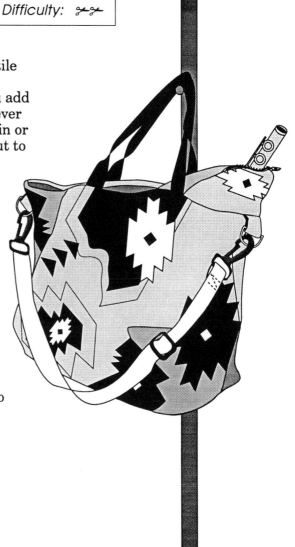

How to Make an Expandable Zippered Tote

You'll Need (for one 20"×14"×6" bag)

Fabric: 1 yd. each of fabric and lining, at least 44" wide

Optional: 1 yd. fusible interfacing, at least 44" wide (for light- to medium-weight fabrics)

Notions: one 20" dress zipper

1¼ yd. of 1" webbing for short handles or 1¾ yd. for long handles

Optional: one 9" dress zipper, chalk or other marker, and ruler (for hidden pocket; see Option 1, pages 46–47)

Optional: two D- or web-rings, two snaphooks (swivel or plain), one slider—all 1"—and an additional 1¾ yd. webbing (for shoulder strap; see Option 2, page 47)

1. Prepare fabric

a. Cut one panel each of fabric and lining 21"×36"; cut two panels each of fabric and lining 21"×7". (*Tip:* Cut all 21" edges on crosswise grain.) (*Note:* If using a directional print, create large panel by cutting two rectangles of fabric 21"×18½"; stitch them together using a ½" seam allowance, with print correctly positioned on each side.)

b. Trim ¼" from both length and width of large lining panel, to allow for the turn of the cloth.

c. *Optional:* For light- and medium-weight fabrics, cut a third set of panels, of fusible interfacing. Fuse interfacing to fabric, according to manufacturer's directions. (*Tip:* Test first, using scraps of fabric and interfacing.)

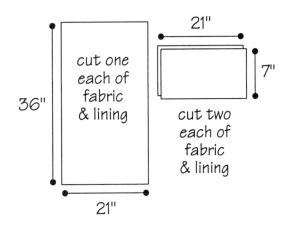

cut one each of fabric & lining

36"

21"

21"

7"

cut two each of fabric & lining

2. Sew zippered extension

a. Place zipper tape along edge of one of the small fabric panels, right sides together. Place one small lining panel over zipper, right side of lining to zipper (so zipper is sandwiched between fabric and lining). Align edges; pin. Stitch through all three layers, about ⅛" from zipper teeth. Press or finger-press fabric and lining away from zipper.

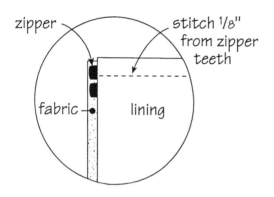

b. Repeat Step 2a for remaining edge of zipper tape.

c. Edgestitch from right side through all layers, beginning and ending 1" from edges of fabric.

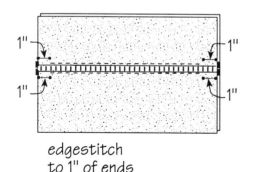

edgestitch
to 1" of ends

d. Fold extension so fabric and lining panels are right sides together. At center, fold zipper in half, right sides together, with lining seam allowances toward fabric. Stitch through all layers on both sides, over zipper ends, using a scant ½" seam allowance. Finger-press seams open.

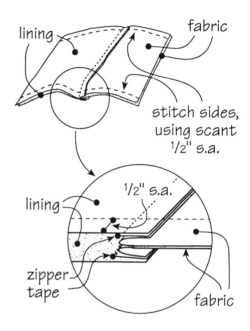

Tip: Unzip zipper a few inches for easier stitching. Also, be careful not to stitch over zipper teeth or stops.

e. Turn extension right side out. Open zipper. Baste or serge raw edges together.

3. Sew body and lining

a. Fold fabric panel in half, right sides together, matching raw edges. Stitch or serge side seams, using a scant ⅜" seam allowance. *Optional:* Clean-finish edges if not serged.

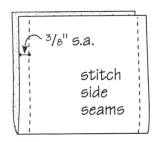

3/8" s.a.

stitch side seams

b. To create bottom, flatten one corner to make a triangular point, aligning side seam with center bottom. Mark a 6"-long line perpendicular to seam, 3" in from point; stitch along line.

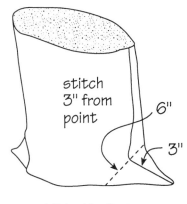

stitch 3" from point

6"

3"

c. Stitch or serge ⅛" inside first seam, toward point, to reinforce. If stitched, trim seam allowance to ¼"; clean-finish if desired. Repeat for other corner. (*Tip:* Press or finger-press both side-seam allowances in the same direction before stitching, e.g., both pointing toward front.)

d. Repeat Steps 3a through 3c for lining.

e. Slip lining inside fabric, wrong sides together, matching raw edges and aligning side seams so that fabric and lining seam allowances are facing in opposite directions (to reduce bulk). Pin. Baste or serge around top, using a ½" seam allowance. (*Tip:* Ease fabric to lining by stitching with lining on top, next to presser foot; friction from foot will help stretch lining to fit.)

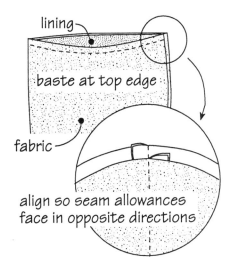

lining

baste at top edge

fabric

align so seam allowances face in opposite directions

4. Attach handles and extension

a. Cut webbing in half. *Optional:* Clean-finish ends (stitch or bind cotton; sear polypropylene and nylon) to prevent fraying.

b. Turn bag inside out. Mark webbing placement lines with pins on right side of fabric, 3" to either side of front and back centers.

c. Position one piece of webbing just beyond placement lines on front, with ends extending a scant ½" beyond raw edges of fabric. (*Note:* Be sure handle is not twisted.) Pin or baste. Repeat for back.

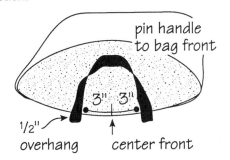

pin handle to bag front

3" 3"

½" overhang

center front

d. Slip zippered extension inside bag body, right sides together. Pin, matching raw edges and side seams. Stitch ⅝" from edge.

5. Finish bag

a. Turn bag right side out. Press seam allowance to one side. Fold extension to inside along seamline; press. Edgestitch.

b. Stitch again ⅜" from edgestitching.

c. Stitch again ⅜" from second stitching line.

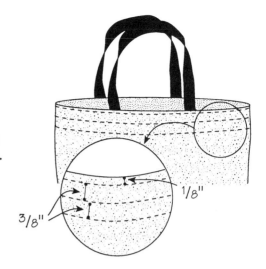

3/8"

1/8"

Options, Ideas & Variations...

1 Add a hidden pocket behind the extension. To do this, you'll need a 9" dress zipper, a 7" × 12" backing panel (cut from lining fabric), and a 1½" × 12" strip of fusible interfacing.

Construct bag through Step 1. Before proceeding with Step 2, install the hidden pocket:

a. Center interfacing strip on one extension lining panel; fuse in place,

fuse interfacing strip
to lining panel

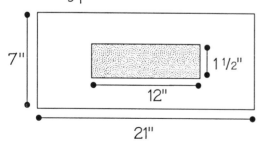

7"

1 1/2"

12"

21"

according to the manufacturer's directions.

b. Draw a ½" × 9" rectangle in center of interfaced area; cut down the middle, to within ¼" of ends; clip to each corner.

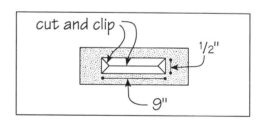

cut and clip

1/2"

9"

c. Turn raw edges of opening to inside (WST); press. Center zipper under "window," right sides up; edgestitch in place.

d. Clean-finish 7"-long edges of backing panel; stitch it to the lining, centered behind the zipper, to finish the pocket.

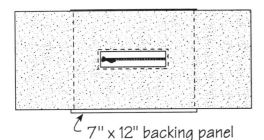

7" x 12" backing panel

2 Add an adjustable shoulder strap. For this variation, you'll need an additional 1¾ yards of 1" webbing, plus the following 1" hardware: two D- or web-rings, two snaphooks (swivel or plain), and one slider.

a. Complete construction through Step 4c.

b. Cut two 3" pieces of webbing (from the additional length). *Optional:* Clean-finish ends of webbing.

c. Loop one short piece of webbing through a D- or web-ring; fold in half. Center ends over each side seam, aligning raw edges. Pin or baste. Repeat for remaining ring.

stitch D-rings to side seams

d. Continue with Step 4d to finish the bag.

e. Loop one end of webbing around center bar of slider; stitch to secure.

f. Thread one snaphook onto webbing, with hook to right side of webbing.

g. Thread raw end of webbing through slider. Thread remaining snaphook onto end; stitch to secure.

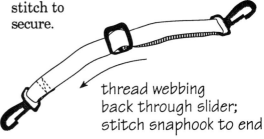

thread webbing back through slider; stitch snaphook to end

h. Clip snaphooks to D- or web-rings on tote bag.

Victorian Carpetbag

Difficulty: ✂

Large travel bags made of carpetlike fabric were quite popular in the last third of the nineteenth century. Today, "carpetbags" have largely been supplanted by the modern suitcase, but their memory lives on in that term so familiar from high-school history class: "the carpetbaggers." (In case you, too, are searching without success through old, faded memory banks, I just looked it up: The carpetbaggers were Northerners who, lured by the economic promise of Reconstruction, traveled south after the Civil War to make their fortunes. They were so named because they were reputed to carry all their possessions in one large carpetbag.)

Though it may not accommodate everything you own, this sturdy bag—reminiscent of its Victorian-era namesake—will hold plenty. It's a perfect carry-on for plane or train, large enough to hold an overnight wardrobe or to stow the many odds and ends you need when traveling with children . . . with room to spare to handle the inevitable "overflow" on the return trip.

How to Make a Victorian Carpetbag

You'll Need (for one 17"×14"×8" bag)

Fabric: ⅝ yd. heavyweight tapestry fabric, at least 54" wide (more if fabric has a dominant motif; see Step 1a)

1⅛ yd. lining fabric, at least 36" wide

¼ yd. medium-weight fusible knit interfacing

Notions: eight ⅜" grommets and grommet-setting tool (optional, see note in Step 4a)

eight 1½-yd. lengths of ⅛" or ³⁄₁₆" leather, suede, or decorative cording* (all the same, or mixed colors and widths)

* Some possibilities: ⅛" rattail cord, rawhide bootlaces, or precut strips from a leather retailer. As of this writing, Tandy carries 18 different colors of "suede lace" in its catalog, available in 25-yd. rolls by mail or by the yard at their stores. Fabric stores may carry suede lace, too, but generally in only a few colors.

1. Prepare fabric

a. Cut two panels of tapestry fabric, 21½"×27". (*Note:* If fabric has a dominant motif, be sure it is centered on each panel before cutting. Consider this when purchasing your fabric; you may need to buy more than ⅝ yard, particularly for fabrics with very large motifs.)

b. Cut lining to 35½"×26¾".

c. Cut two strips of interfacing, each 4½"×26". Fuse one to wrong side of each top edge of tapestry panels,

cut tapestry fabric into two panels, with motif centered on each

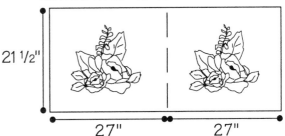

21 1/2"
27" 27"

according to manufacturer's directions.

d. *Optional:* Clean-finish raw edges.

---

2. Sew bag and lining

a. Stitch tapestry panels together at bottom, right sides together, with edges slightly offset, using a ½" seam allowance (check to be sure motifs are positioned properly before stitching).

stitch bottom with panels slightly offset

½" s.a.

b. Press seam allowances to one side, with wider side covering narrower one. Topstitch from right side, ⅜" from seamline.

c. Fold tapestry panel in half, right sides together, matching edges. Stitch both side seams, using ½" seam allowance. Press seam allowances open.

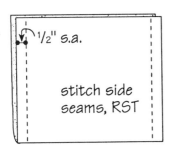

½" s.a.

stitch side seams, RST

d. To create bottom, flatten one corner to make a triangular point, aligning side seam with center bottom. Mark an 8"-long line perpendicular to seam, 4" in from point; stitch along line. Stitch again ⅛" from first stitching line, toward point, to reinforce. Repeat for other corner. *Optional:* Stitch again

about 1" from corners and trim off tips to reduce bulk.

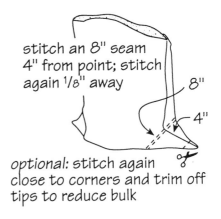

stitch an 8" seam 4" from point; stitch again ⅛" away

8"

4"

optional: stitch again close to corners and trim off tips to reduce bulk

e. *Optional:* Sew a patch pocket to right side of lining panel, centered about 1½" from one short edge of fabric.

f. Repeat Steps 2c and 2d for lining panel, leaving a 7" opening in one side seam, about 5" from top edge.

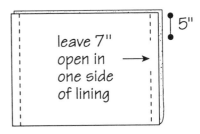

leave 7" open in one side of lining

5"

3. Assemble bag

a. Press under 2" at top of bag, wrong sides together, to mark foldline.

b. Turn lining right side out. Slip lining into bag. Unfold top edge of bag. Pin lining to bag, right sides together, matching edges and side seams. Stitch or serge around top edge, ½" from edge of fabric.

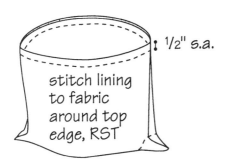

stitch lining
to fabric
around top
edge, RST

½" s.a.

c. Turn bag right side out through opening in lining. Edgestitch opening shut.

d. Smooth lining inside bag, folding top edge along pressed foldline (Step 3a); corner "triangles" should all be folded toward bottom. Press lining flat at seamline around top of bag. Topstitch 1½" from folded edge to secure.

e. *Optional:* Stitch in the ditch along side-bottom ("triangle") seamlines, through all layers, to secure lining to tapestry fabric.

4. Finish bag

a. Mark positions for grommets 1¾" and 8½" on either side of both seamlines. Cut holes at marks; set grommets, following manufacturer's directions.

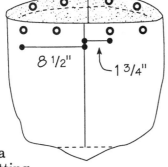

8 ½"

1 ¾"

Note: If you don't want to invest in a grommet-setting tool, you can usually hire out the service. Check your yellow pages under "Boat Covers, Tops & Upholstery." Prices and sizes vary, so call first; I found that most places in my city will set ⅜" grommets for 50¢ to $1 each.

b. Braid together four lengths of leather, suede, or cording; repeat for remaining four strips. (See instructions for four-strand braiding on page 52.)

Alternatively: Purchase 2½ yards of ¼" to ⅜" decorative cording, leather rope, decorative chain, or whatever, and cut in half to use for handles.

c. Thread the end (untie knot and tape tightly if necessary) of one braid through a grommet nearest to a side seam, threading from outside to inside of bag. Moving away from side seam toward center of bag, thread braid back out through next grommet, then in again through the next and finally out through the grommet nearest the side seam opposite from where you started.

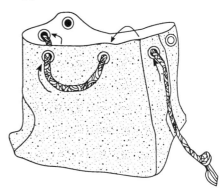

d. Repeat Step 4c for remaining braid.

e. Lay bag flat. Stretch cords flat, an equal length at each end. Knot close to side seams. Unbraid rope below knots.

Four-Strand Braiding

Make an interesting handle for your Victorian Carpetbag using four-strand braiding. This technique produces a rounded rope. When different colors are incorporated into the same braid, a spiral or striped effect can result, depending on the number and order of the colors used.

As a rule of thumb, the finished diameter of the braid will be about twice the diameter of the strands used to make it. For example, four ⅛" cords will produce a braid that is about ¼" in diameter. In terms of finished length, count on losing about 25 percent of your original length to "shrinkage." Of course, both these guidelines will vary based on how tightly you braid and on how stiff or supple the cord is to begin with.

To braid:

- Tape or knot the four strands together at one end.

- Secure the end to a stationary object (e.g., tie it to a doorknob, pin it to a chair or ironing board, clamp it in a vice), so you can put a little tension on the rope as you braid, to make the process easier and the product more uniform.

- Begin with the strand farthest to the right. Bring it under the two middle strands (1), then up and over the strand that is now immediately to its right (2).

- Take the strand farthest to the left. Bring it under the two middle strands (3), then up and over the strand that is now immediately to its left (4).

- Continue this sequence—alternating the far-right and far-left strands, always bringing them under two and then back-tracking over one—to the end.

- To secure, tape or knot the ends.

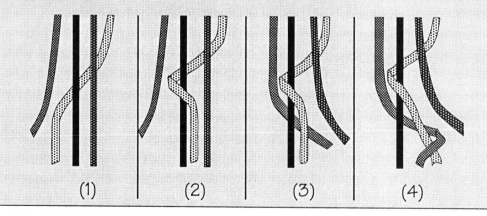

(1)   (2)   (3)   (4)

3

Duffels

Duffels are among the most common and the most versatile of bag forms. Cylindrical in shape, they take their name from the utilitarian "duffel" cloth from which they were first made. The cloth, in turn, takes its name (as so many fabrics do) from the city where it was originally manufactured: seventeenth-century Duffel, in Belgium near Antwerp. There is disagreement about whether the original duffel cloth was made from wool or linen; in any event, it was certainly a coarse cloth with a thick nap.

Duffel bags fall into two types: open or closed. Both are constructed by stitching a rectangle of fabric into a cylinder, then inserting a circle of fabric at one (open) or both (closed) ends.

The open duffel is generally carried or worn with the circular panel at bottom and the open end up; this hole is closed via a drawstring—either within a casing or run through grommets—around the top edge. In contrast, the closed duffel is most frequently carried with the circular panels at the sides and features a zipper that runs the length of the rectangular panel, from one circular end to the other.

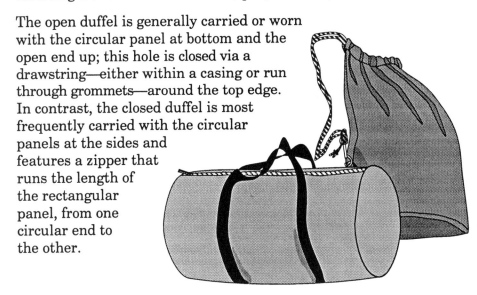

Project 12

Leather String Duffel

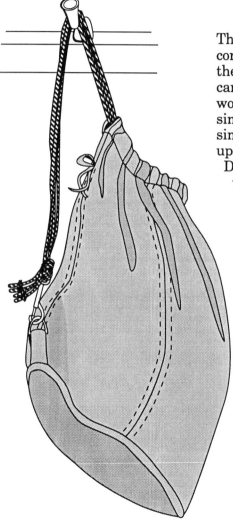

The difficulty of this bag is not in the construction—that part is easy. Rather, the four-scissors rating reflects the extra care and planning that is required when working with leather. Leather gives this simple open-duffle shape a classy look (a similar bag was recently featured in an upscale ready-made catalog, sporting the DKNY label and a price tag closing in on the $300 mark). Lining fabric, treated as interlining, provides stability as well as a nice finish on the inside. A zipper set into the side seam allows easy access, even while you're wearing it. Of course, you may choose to make this classic duffel in a fabric more familiar and forgiving than real leather, in which case, it'll sew up in a snap!

If you decide to give real leather a try, read through "Sewing with Leather" on page 55 before you begin. Take the time to understand and apply these basic principles, and you'll have no trouble sewing this special fabric.

Sewing with Leather

Leather is a "fabric" with which many experienced sewers have little familiarity. Its relative expense ($2/sq. ft. and up), the fact that it's not sold in fabric stores, and its irregular shape make sewing with it, if not downright intimidating then at least an adventure! Keep a few simple guidelines in mind as you sew, and your leather experience will be a happy one.

Tips for cutting and sewing leather

• Leather is irregular in shape. Take your pattern pieces with you to the leather store to figure out what you need, and keep in mind the following when laying out your pieces.

• Leather is inherently "imperfect." For best results, use a single-layer cutting layout, selecting the specific areas of the skin that are most suitable for each particular piece. To do this, cut a separate pattern for every piece you need. Waxed paper is a good choice for this; it allows you to see through to the leather, to position the pattern pieces in a way that avoids holes and blemishes.

• Leather has a "grainline" along the backbone. Cut pieces along the backbone for minimal stretch. Also, hides are usually thickest near the neck area and thinnest near the legs areas. Place your pattern pieces accordingly.

• Do not pin. Mark lightly around pattern pieces with chalk, or use pattern weights. For seams, use gluestick or paper clips (vinyl-covered ones work well) instead of pins to secure layers before stitching. Pinning leaves permanent holes and weakens the fabric.

• Do not rip. Make every attempt to stitch it right the first time. Also, do not backstitch to begin and end seams; instead, tie off thread ends. Stitching, like pinning, leaves permanent holes and weakens the fabric.

• Leather disintegrates natural fibers. Work with polyester thread, linings, and cordings.

• Leather, particularly lightweight types, stretches. Use an even-feed foot or a Teflon foot when stitching, or place a piece of tissue paper between the leather and the throatplate, and between the leather and the foot.

• Lengthen the stitch length: Because stitching perforates the leather, the fewer stitches the better. Set stitch length for 8 to 10 stitches per inch.

• Test! Before beginning stitching, test your thread and needle(s) on the leather you've chosen. For lightweight leathers, a size 12/80 or 14/90 universal-point needle will usually work best; for heavyweight leathers, a leather needle may be required.

How to Make a Leather String Duffel

You'll Need (for one 16" × 11" bag)

Fabric:	approximately 13 sq. ft. of lightweight leather, such as pigskin suede
	1 yd. polyester lining fabric, at least 45" wide
	12" square of fusible knit interfacing
Notions:	3½ yd. of ¼" or ⅜" decorative cording for handle
	one 12" dress zipper
	1 yd. stiff cording for welting (such as traverse cord)
	one ½" brass or silver snaphook (swivel or plain)
	one ⅝" brass or silver D-ring (to match snaphook)
	gluestick, paper clips, chalk
	Optional: 1⅛ yd. of ¾" twill tape (to finish seam allowance around inside bottom)

1. Prepare fabric

a. Cut pattern pieces for leather from waxed paper:

- one 12" circle
- four 10" × 18" rectangles
- one 1½" × 36¼" strip
- one ¾" × 3" rectangle
- one ¾" × 6½" rectangle
- one 1½" square

b. Lay pattern pieces on leather, avoiding blemishes, holes, and thin or weak spots; position circle over thickest area (near neck) if possible. Mark around patterns with chalk or use pattern weights. Cut out pieces, using a rotary cutter and ruler for straight edges, if available.

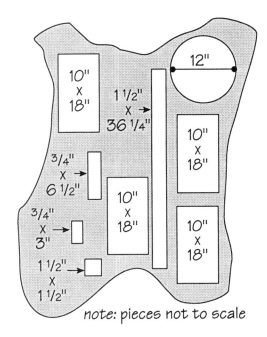

note: pieces not to scale

c. From lining, cut:
- one 11¾" circle
- four 9¾" × 17¾" rectangles

d. From fusible knit interfacing, cut:
- one 11¾" circle

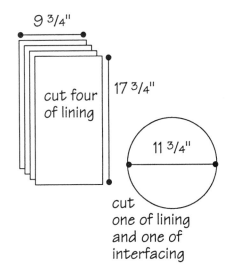

9 ¾"

cut four of lining

17 ¾"

cut one of lining and one of interfacing

11 ¾"

e. *Optional:* Serge, zigzag, or pink to clean-finish edges of lining pieces.

f. Fuse interfacing to lining circle, wrong sides together, according to manufacturer's directions. *Optional:* Fuse rough-cut 12" circle (or square) of interfacing to lining before cutting 11¾" circle.

g. Glue four lining rectangles to corresponding leather panels, wrong sides together, using light strokes of gluestick around all edges, and matching edges exactly. (*Note:* Leather will be slightly larger than lining panels, to allow for turn of the cloth.)

h. Apply gluestick to wrong side of 36¼" strip of leather. Center stiff cording along length. Fold strip in half to cover cording; press firmly to make welting. (*Tip:* Work in sections, gluing 8" to 10" at a time.)

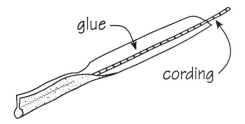

glue

cording

2. Insert zipper

a. Stitch two side panels, right sides together, using a ½" seam allowance and a long stitch length (8 to 10 stitches per inch), leaving openings for casing and zipper as indicated in the following drawing. Finger-press seam open from wrong side.

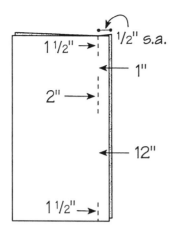

1 1/2" →
1/2" s.a.
← 1"
2" →
← 12"
1 1/2" →

zipper tape to seam allowance, ⅛" from zipper teeth, using zipper foot. Repeat for other side.

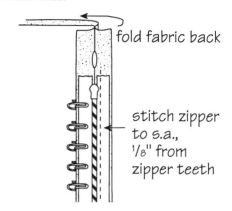

fold fabric back

stitch zipper to s.a., ⅛" from zipper teeth

b. Position zipper on seam allowance within 12" opening, with zipper pull at top and zipper stop at bottom, right sides together (so pull sticks through opening to right side of bag), matching edges of zipper tape and fabric; paper-clip zipper to seam allowances to secure.

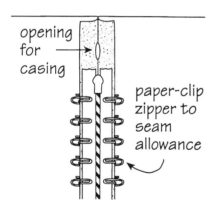

opening for casing

paper-clip zipper to seam allowance

c. Fold fabric back, so seam allowance can be placed under presser foot. Stitch

d. Topstitch from right side, ¼" on either side of seamline and across bottom of zipper (at end of opening). (*Note:* Be careful not to stitch across zipper stop.) Tie-off thread ends.

3. Reinforce casing opening

a. Fold 6½" strip under 1¼" at one end; glue end lightly to secure, leaving loop open.

b. Center strip over seam, matching top edges, with loop overlapping top of zipper. Stitch a "Z" just above zipper stop, through all layers.

c. Determine where strip covers opening in seam (for casing); mark placement with chalk. (*Tip:* This is easiest to do by folding the strip back and marking the wrong side.) Cut a narrow window in strip at mark, ⅛" × ¾". Center window over seamline opening; glue down lightly, if desired. Edgestitch along edges and around window.

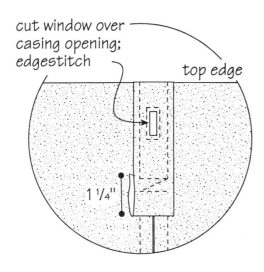

cut window over casing opening; edgestitch

top edge

1 1/4"

5. Stitch bag body and casing

a. Stitch remaining large panels together (forming a cylinder), right sides together, using ½" seam allowances. Finger-press seams open. Topstitch ¼" from either side of all seamlines. (*Tip:* Complete the stitch-press-topstitch sequence for one panel at a time, so you can work in the flat until the very last seam.)

b. Turn under 1½" at top edge; paper-clip to secure. Stitch 1" from edge to form casing. Stitch again 1¼" from edge.

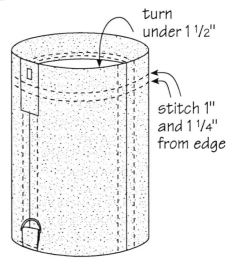

turn under 1 1/2"

stitch 1" and 1 1/4" from edge

4. Attach D-ring

a. Thread 3" strip of leather through D-ring; fold in half, with D-ring at loop end.

b. Center strip over seamline at bottom, raw edges even. Stitch ¼" from bottom edge of bag, through all layers.

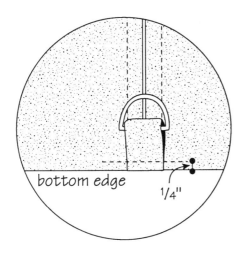

bottom edge

1/4"

6. Attach bottom

a. Eighth-mark bottom edge of bag. (*Tip:* Use seamlines for quarters, then cut a small notch midway between each for eighths.)

b. Eighth-mark bottom of circle. (*Tip:* Fold circle into eighths, and barely notch edge at each fold.)

c. Turn bag body inside out. Glue welting around right side of bottom edge, raw edges even. At joint, trim excess welting and butt ends; glue 1½" square snugly around welting to cover joint.

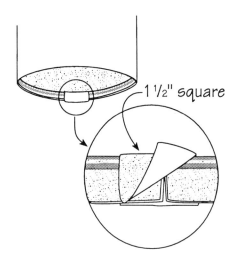

1 ½" square

d. Paper-clip bottom to bag over welting, matching notches, right sides together and raw edges even. Stitch with zipper foot as close to cording as possible.

e. *Optional:* Clean-finish seam allowance: wrap ¾" twill tape around edge and zigzag to secure.

7. Finish bag

a. Turn bag right side out. *Optional zipper pull:* Cut a ⅛" × 5" strip of leather. Fold in half. Thread loop through hole in zipper tab; thread ends through loop and pull tight to secure.

b. Fold decorative cord in half; thread loop end through casing.

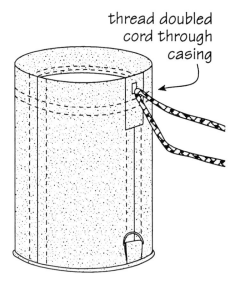

thread doubled cord through casing

c. Tie all four cords to swivel snaphook; cut loop and knot ends individually. Clip snaphook to D-ring.

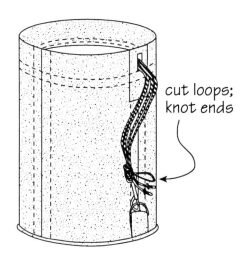

cut loops; knot ends

Options, Ideas & Variations...

1 Mix and match. Choose a bold ethnic print fabric for the body, and accent it with leather, Ultraleather, or Fabu-Leather bands topstitched around top and bottom.

2 Use grommets around the top edge, rather than a casing, for the drawstring.

3 Skip the seaming, and make the bag from a single panel (cut it 37" × 18").

4 Substitute a strap handle stitched directly to the back seam, with a buckle closure for adjustability.

5 Add a second D-ring at bottom—about a panel's width away from the first—and an extra snaphook; use the second set when you want to wear the bag backpack-style.

Project 13

Huge Quilted Duffel

Difficulty: ✐✐✐

This is probably the bag that most people today associate with the word *duffel:* round ends, a zippered closure across the top, and web strap handles. The similarity of this bag to other zippered duffels ends there, though. This one is *really* big: a whopping yard long and almost half-a-yard high. And it includes a detachable shoulder strap.

How many times have you packed for a day with the family at the lake or on the slopes, and had to juggle eight or ten small bags to pack it all in? Or how do your kids arrive for sleep overs and camp-outs? With five or six assorted parcels in tow, right?

And sports: anyone with a budding goalie or linebacker in the family knows the sheer volume of stuff to be carted from home to practice to game, week after week. The Huge Quilted Duffel is the answer: a convenient alternative to stringing bags and bundles all over your body, like lights on a Christmas tree. This one bag holds everything.

The instructions that follow are for making one from a quilt-it-yourself fabric, to give you the greatest amount of versatility. Quilting gives even the lightest-weight fashion fabric the body it needs for so large a bag. Or you can skip the quilting, and make the bag out of either pre-quilted or heavy-weight fabric. Choose 1,000-denier Cordura, for instance, and you've got the supersize sports bag so popular with athletes of all ages—without the supersize price tag.

How to Make a Huge Quilted Duffel

You'll Need (for one 35"×16" bag)

Fabric: 2 yd. each of fabric and low-loft (thin) quilt batting, 44" wide (1½ yd. each if 54" or wider)

2⅜ yd. lining fabric, 44" wide

one 24"×11" piece of contrasting fabric (for pocket; if making pocket *and* welting from contrasting fabric, ¾ yd. of 44"-wide fabric)

Optional, for light- or medium-weight fabrics: 2 yd. of heavywight fusible interfacing, such as Pellon Decor-Bond

Notions: 1 yd. #5 zipper tape and one zipper pull

2⅞ yd. of ⅜" to ½" welting (or 2⅞ yd. cording and extra fabric to make your own; see above for yardage)

11" of ½" elastic

5 yd. of 1½" webbing

1½" hardware: two web- or D-rings, two snaphooks (swivel or plain), one slider

several dozen safety pins

Optional: one 1½" shoulder pad (for webbing—see Glossary)

Optional: 3 yd. of ¾" twill tape (to bind seam allowances)

1. Prepare fabric

a. Cut one rectangle of fabric and batting, 50¾"× 36"; cut one of lining about 1" larger all around. Cut two circles each of fabric and batting 17" in diameter; cut two of lining about 1" larger all around. (*Note:* Accuracy in cutting batting and lining is not crucial; they will be trimmed to size later.)

b. Cut one rectangle each of contrasting fabric and lining for pocket, 24"× 11".

c. *Optional:* Cut interfacing pieces ¼" smaller than fabric all around. Fuse interfacing to fabric, according to manufacturer's directions. (*Tip:* Test on scraps before fusing.)

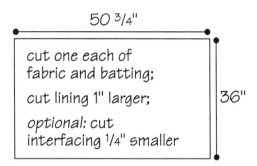

50 ³/₄"

cut one each of fabric and batting;

cut lining 1" larger;

optional: cut interfacing ¹/₄" smaller

36"

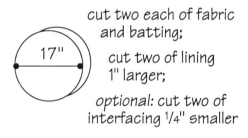

cut two each of fabric and batting;

cut two of lining 1" larger;

optional: cut two of interfacing ¹/₄" smaller

17"

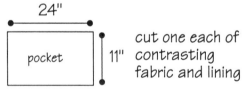

24"

pocket

11"

cut one each of contrasting fabric and lining

2. Quilt fabric

Note: If you've never done freehand machine quilting before, see next page for techniques and tips.

a. Place lining, wrong side up, on flat surface. Tape (e.g., to a floor), clip (e.g., to a table), or pin (e.g., into a carpet) to surface, stretching slightly so lining is moderately taut.

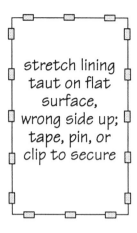

stretch lining taut on flat surface, wrong side up; tape, pin, or clip to secure

b. Place batting over lining; smooth from center out. Place fabric, right side up, over batting and lining. Smooth from center out.

c. Pin- or thread-baste layers together, every 4"–6", beginning in center and working toward edges. (*Tip:* For small pieces, such as circular ends, straight pins are fine; for larger pieces, use safety pins so it doesn't feel like you're wrestling a porcupine while quilting.)

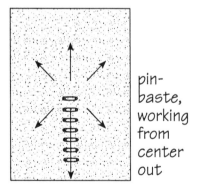

pin-baste, working from center out

d. Trim edges of batting to ½" less than edges of fabric.

Freehand Machine Quilting

If you've never tried freehand machine quilting, you're in for a treat. It's fun and easy and useful for so many sewing applications, from quilts to clothing to home dec. A bag is the perfect place to begin, too. It's fairly small, so your time commitment is limited. Plus, if you make a mistake, it will be far less noticeable than one made front and center on a garment (where it inevitably *would* be).

Anything goes, as far as your designs for machine quilting. Follow the pattern in your fabric, doodle, write your name, or mark a pattern and follow the lines (use chalk or some other nondamaging, easily removeable marker). With freehand quilting, *you* move the fabric under the needle, rather than the presser foot/feed dogs pulling it through. That gives you lots of freedom in design and allows you to stitch in any direction.

Tips for machine quilting:

• Practice. Begin each session working on a piece of scrap fabric, to loosen up your arms and hands. Because stitch length depends on you moving the fabric under the needle, you need to develop a feel for how far and how fast to move the material to create uniform stitches. Keep your muscles relaxed, and don't forget to breathe!

• For all but the smallest quilts, enlarge the flat surface around the sewing machine (push up card tables or move the sewing machine to a larger table). One of the biggest sources of frustration and difficulty is the sheer bulk of the fabric spilling over the table, pulling and dragging against you as you work.

• Low-loft (thin) battings are easiest to machine quilt—the best choice for beginners.

• Be sure the lining is taut before placing and basting the batting and fabric on top. This will help you keep from stitching tucks into the lining as you quilt.

• Work from the center out. This applies equally to pin-basting and stitching.

• Make a "hoop" with your hands around the section you're working on, or pinch to grab a firm hold on either side; stretch slightly to keep layers taut as you stitch. Work on small sections at a time. Stitch in place a few times to begin and end a line of stitching.

• Quilt the surface evenly, to keep the overall dimensions uniform. The more stitching you do in an area, the stiffer and smaller that section will become.

• To stitch the center, fold or roll one side of the quilt in to the center; place this rolled portion under the head of the sewing machine; unroll as needed to work toward the side edge. Repeat for the other side.

e. Adjust machine for freehand quilting: lower feed dogs, release pressure on presser foot, install darning foot, and change needle if necessary (generally, a size 12/80 or 14/90 is appropriate).

f. Quilt to within ¼" of fabric edges, working from the center out.

g. Trim excess lining even with edges of fabric. Clean-finish raw edges.

3. Install pocket

a. Stitch or serge pocket fabric to lining along one long edge, right sides together. Press seam allowance toward lining.

b. Fold, wrong sides together, with fabric showing ¾" above lining on back. Stitch in the ditch to form casing. Clean-finish bottom edge, trimming excess lining close to fabric.

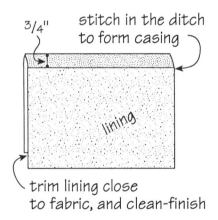

c. Mark two points at bottom edge, 3" in from each side. Trim pocket diagonally, from marks to top corners on each side.

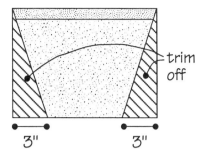

d. Pleat bottom to 12" wide, by stacking two ¾" pleats about 1" from each side. Baste.

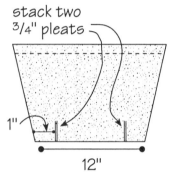

e. Turn under ½" at bottom edge; press. Edgestitch bottom edge of pocket to bag, centered 8" down from one top edge. Stitch again ¼" away.

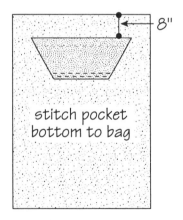

f. Insert 11"-piece of elastic into casing; pin ends to secure. Pin pocket sides to bag, perpendicular to side edges of bag; baste.

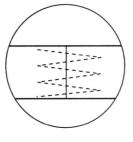

insert elastic; baste sides to bag

4. Prepare webbing

a. Cut 3½ yards of webbing. Clean-finish ends (sear nylon and polypropylene; stitch or fold under cotton and blends).

Butt ends together snugly; stitch back and forth several times to secure. (*Note:* Be sure webbing isn't twisted before stitching ends together.)

b. Quarter-mark webbing, using butt joint as one of the four marks.

c. Measure and mark 6" to either side of two opposite quarter marks (this will define two 12" segments, for the handles).

d. Fold webbing in half lengthwise along each 12" segment. Edgestitch to form handles.

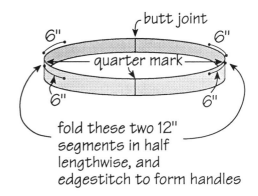

butt joint

6" 6"

quarter mark

6" 6"

fold these two 12" segments in half lengthwise, and edgestitch to form handles

5. Apply webbing

Mark center bottom line midway across width of bag. Position webbing on right side of fabric, with butt joint and opposite quarter mark on center bottom line, overlapping pocket raw edges ½". (*Note:* Handles will loop over ends of panel.) Pin. Edgestitch webbing to fabric, to about 5" from each end.

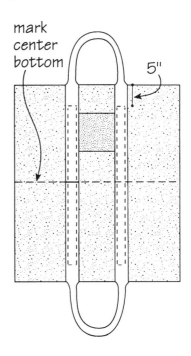

mark center bottom

5"

6. Install zipper

a. Stitch one side of zipper tape to one top edge of bag, right sides together, about ⅛" from zipper teeth. Repeat for other side.

stitch zipper to fabric,
RST, ⅛" from teeth

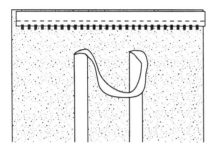

b. Edgestitch from right side.

c. Slide zipper pull onto zipper tape.

7. Sew sides

a. Cut two 4" pieces of webbing; clean-finish ends (sear or stitch). Loop one through each web-ring (or D-ring). Fold webbing in half; baste to right side of fabric, raw edges aligned, centered over each end of zipper.

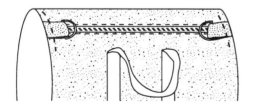

b. *Optional:* Make your own welting (102").

c. Turn bag wrong side out. Baste welting to right side of each side edge, raw edges even, beginning and ending 2" from each end of welting. At joint, trim excess welting and butt ends.

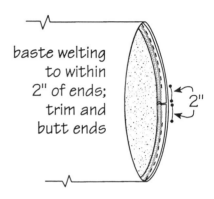

baste welting
to within
2" of ends;
trim and
butt ends

d. Cut a 2" bias square of scrap fabric; turn sides under ½", and wrap snugly around welting to cover joint. Finish stitching welting to fabric, over scrap.

2" square

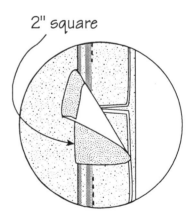

e. Eighth-mark side edges of bag. Eighth-mark circles. Pin circles to sides, matching raw edges and eighth marks. Stitch as close to cording as possible. (*Tip:* Stitch with bag body [rather than circle ends] on top, under presser foot.) Stitch again ¼" away, within seam allowance, to reinforce.

f. *Optional:* Bind seam allowances with twill tape.

8. Sew detachable shoulder strap

a. Clean-finish ends of remaining length (approx. 1⅜ yards) of webbing (sear or stitch).

b. Loop one end of webbing around center bar of slider; stitch to secure. Thread one snaphook onto webbing, with hook to right side of webbing.

c. Thread other end of webbing through slider, over stitched loop. Thread shoulder pad onto webbing. Thread remaining snaphook onto end; stitch to secure.

d. Clip snaphooks to web-rings (or D-rings) on bag.

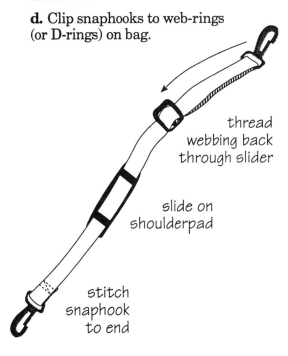

thread webbing back through slider

slide on shoulderpad

stitch snaphook to end

Options, Ideas & Variations...

1 Small zippered duffels, lined with vinyl or waterproof nylon and minus the strap handles, are great for taking makeup or toiletries to the gym.

2 Make a tiny, color-blocked duffel just the right size for kids' pencils.

3 Make a zippered duffel in any size. To determine cutting dimensions, use this formula:

- The cutting diameter for circles will be the finished diameter plus 1" for seam allowances (e.g., for finished ends that are 5½" in diameter, cut 6½" circles).

- The cutting width for the rectangular panel will be the finished width plus 1" for seam allowances (e.g., for a 12" finished width, cut rectangle 13" wide).

- To figure the cutting length for the rectangular panel, multiply the finished diameter of the circles by pi (3.14) and add 1" for seam allowances (e.g., for a bag with ends that are a finished 5½" in diameter, cut a rectangle 18¼" long [(5½" × 3.14) + 1" = 18¼"]).

4 Super Sports Bag: Choose a substantial outdoor-type fabric, such as 1,000-denier Cordura. Lined or unlined, this bag is both popular and practical for athletes of all ages . . . and—given the large price tags on most commercial models—it's one that will surely be appreciated for years to come. Add pockets inside and/or outside to suit your own sports star's needs. This is a

great coach's bag, too, or a handy storage bag for keeping bats and balls together at home.

5 Change the shape of the ends; they don't always have to be circles! Try long or wide triangles, squares, rectangles, and trapezoids. How about a medium-size bag in a trendy jungle-print, for carry-on convenience when traveling? Make it 21" long, with 9" × 12" ends, for perfect under-seat fit on airlines. (To figure the cutting length, measure along the seamline of one endpiece, and add 1" for seam allowances.)

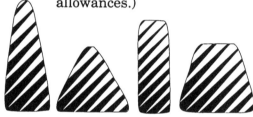

6 Slumber-Party Pack: Pick a playful pair of prints, make a coordinating sleeping bag and pillowcase (see Project 21), and you've got a dynamite kid's sleep-over or camp-out bag!

4

Cases

Cases are much like zippered duffles in form, with two essential differences: For cases, the ends are generally rectangular rather than circular and the zipper runs around the girth of the bag rather than from end to end. The briefcase and the suitcase are probably the most familiar members of this species, but once you understand the form, you'll see that many variations on the theme are possible.

Library Book Bag

Difficulty: ✦✦✦

This is an open-ended variation on the basic briefcase, customized for toting essentials back and forth from the library by the addition of shoulder-length handles, a divider to keep loose papers corralled, plus an inside pocket panel with

spaces for your library card, a notepad, and several pencils and pens. Pick a solid-color fabric for the body, and jazz it up with floral or striped binding. Or maybe you prefer the opposite look: a pretty print bag framed with a bold, solid binding.

Whatever your style, choose a fabric with sufficient body to stand up to the weight of the books you'll be carrying.

The major difficulty in making this bag is that the stiffness and thickness of the heavy fabric makes it hard to maneuver around the curves, particularly when applying the binding. Once you've mastered the construction, though, it's really not a difficult bag to make; you might even consider making one out of leather, for a really classy look.

How to Make a Library Book Bag

You'll Need (for one 17"×13"×3½" bag)

Fabric: 1 yd. heavyweight fabric, 44" or wider (such as denim)

contrasting fabric, 45" or wider, for bias binding and handles (⅝ yd. is sufficient if you piece it; 1⅜ yd. allows you to cut strips to exact length)

½ yd. heavyweight or craft fusible interfacing (such as Pellon Decor-Bond)

Notions: 2¾ yd. of ½" or ¾" belting (for handles)

one gripper snap

bodkin (or a safety pin)

---

1. Prepare fabric

a. Cut rectangles of fabric as follows:

cut fabric:

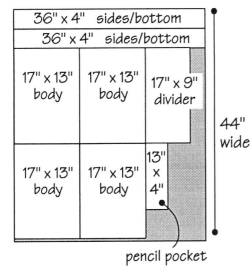

pencil pocket

- two 36"×4" (sides/bottom)
- four 17"×13" (body)
- one 17"×9" (divider)
- one 13"×4" (pencil pocket)

b. Cut interfacing as follows:
- two 16½"×12½" (body)
- one 35½"×3½" (sides/bottom)

c. Cut bias strips from contrasting fabric as follows:

- two 63"×1¾"
- two 4½"×1¾"
- two 50"×2" (for ½" handles) *or* two 50"×2⅝" (for ¾" handles)

d. Curve corners on all body panels and on one long side of divider. (*Tip:* Use a glass or mug to draw curves.) Fuse interfacing to two body panels and to one sides/bottom strip.

---

2. Assemble inside panels

a. Fold under ¼" along straight edge of divider; press. Fold under ¼" again; press. Edgestitch.

b. Pin divider to one of the noninterfaced body panels, right sides up, matching curved corners; baste.

c. Fold under ¼" along both long edges of pencil pocket; press. Fold under ¼" again; press. Edgestitch. Clean-finish short edges. Turn under ⅜" along short edges; press.

d. Mark pencil pocket as indicated:

mark pencil panel:

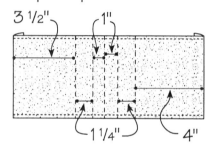

e. Mark remaining noninterfaced body panel as indicated:

mark body panel:

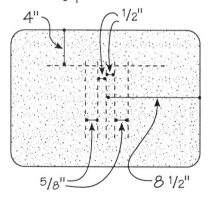

f. Stitch pencil pocket to body as indicated, aligning marks, right sides up. (*Tip:* Use a zipper foot to stitch the narrow pencil pockets.)

apply snap 1 ¼" from top edge

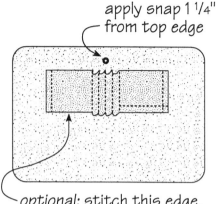

optional: stitch this edge, too, for a pocket rather than a notepad-holder

g. Apply gripper snap, centered, 1¼" down from top edges of each inside panel. (*Tip:* Place or fuse a scrap of fabric or interfacing behind snap to reinforce.)

3. Sew and apply handles

a. *For ¾" handles:* Fold 50" × 2⅝" bias strips in half lengthwise, right sides together; pin closely, or hand baste. Stitch, using a ½" seam allowance. Trim seam allowances to ⅜"; press open.

For ½" handles: Fold 50" × 2" bias strips in half lengthwise, right sides together; pin closely, or hand baste. Stitch, using a scant ½" seam allowance. Trim seam allowances to ¼"; press open.

Tip: When stitching on the bias, use a short stitch length and a just-barely zigzag stitch.

b. Turn tubes right side out; press flat. (*Tip:* Press with seam running down center, rather than along an edge, to distribute bulk evenly.)

c. Cut belting in half. Slide each half into a bias tube, using a bodkin. (*Tip:* Curve the leading end of the belting for easiest insertion.) Smooth fabric over belting, stretching slightly. Trim each to 48"; baste across each end to secure.

d. Position handles on interfaced (or remaining, if none were interfaced) body panels, about 4" from sides, and 2½" from bottom. Edgestitch to within 2" of top; stitch or zigzag between edgestitching at top to reinforce. (*Tip:* Position handles to tilt in slightly— from ¼" to ½"—from bottom to top.)

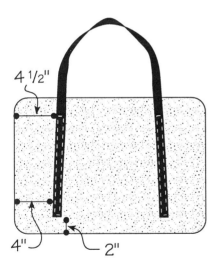

4 1/2"

4"   2"

e. Cover raw ends: stitch a patch, appliqué some scraps, sew on some buttons . . . whatever. (If you're a quilter, you might consider using some mini-quilt blocks or maybe Sunbonnet Sue and Overall Bill.)

4. Assemble bag

a. Stitch or serge one inner to one outer body panel, wrong sides together, ¼" from edges. Repeat for remaining pair of inner/outer body panels. (*Note:* Be sure pencil pocket and divider are facing the right direction relative to handles.)

b. Stitch or serge sides/bottom strips, wrong sides together, ¼" from edges.

c. Bind both short edges of sides/bottom strip with 4½" bias pieces. Trim ends even with fabric.

To apply binding: Stitch binding to fabric, right sides together, raw edges even, a generous ¼" from edge. Wrap binding around raw edge. Turn raw edge of binding under just enough so fold extends about ¹⁄₁₆" beyond first stitching line; pin. Stitch in the ditch from right side, catching folded edge of binding in stitching.

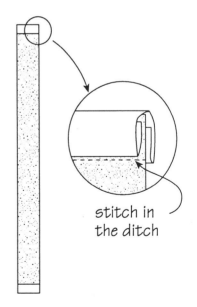

stitch in
the ditch

---

d. Mark center of sides/bottom strip, and a scant 8" to each side of center (these are the corners). Clip seam allowance at all four corners: clip ¼" into strip at each mark and again about ¼" and ½" to each side.

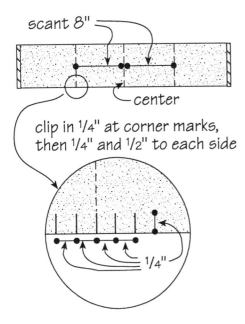

scant 8"

center

clip in ¼" at corner marks, then ¼" and ½" to each side

¼"

e. Mark center bottom of each body panel and centers of each rounded bottom corner.

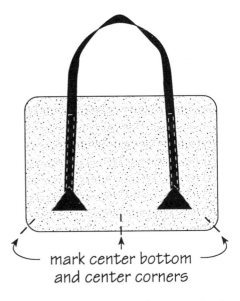

mark center bottom and center corners

f. Pin sides/bottom strip to one body panel, wrong sides together, aligning bottom and corner marks; stitch using a ¼" seam allowance. (*Tip:* Use a zipper foot for easiest stitching.)

g. Apply one 63" bias strip to raw edges, as in Step 4c. (*Tip:* It may be easier to finish the binding by stitching through the fold, from wrong side, rather than stitching in the ditch.)

h. Repeat Steps 4f and 4g for remaining body panel.

Options, Ideas & Variations...

1 Use a purchased handle (see "Sources and Resources" section for mail-order vendors for leather handles and hardware).

3 Make a child-size version for your favorite junior bookworm.

4 Extend the back panel at top so it's long enough to flip over the front, creating a closed bag. You'll have to adjust your stitching of the handle on front to allow clearance for the extension or change the handles to a single strap that attaches at the sides.

2 Add a pocket panel across the front (and the back, too, if you like).

Project 15

Quilter's Carryall

This suitcase-size bag is truly a carryall! It's large enough to fit even the largest quilt-in-progress, and it's got pockets for everything, including a 24"×18" cutting mat, a 24"×6" ruler, a 6"×6" ruler, large and small rotary cutters, two scissors, three shears, eight marking pens and pencils, needles, thread, pins, patterns, templates,

books, magazines, and class notes . . . with room left over to accommodate the overflow.

The Quilter's Carryall features a convenient two-way zipper that runs completely around three sides of the bag—so you can open it up flat, for easy access to all your supplies. Add the optional adjustable shoulder strap to make carrying it all a breeze.

Though no individual element of this bag is difficult to sew, two factors earn it a four-scissors difficulty rating: the large number of pieces (mostly pockets) that must be assembled and its large size, which makes it a bit unwieldy at the sewing machine.

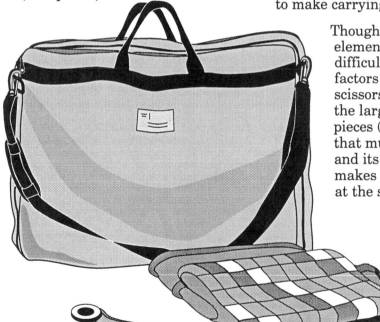

How to Make a Quilter's Carryall

You'll Need (for one 20"×26"×6" bag)

Fabric: 2 yd. sturdy, water-repellent fabric, at least 60" wide (such as coated 1,000-denier Cordura)

Optional: 2¾"×4" piece of clear vinyl (for business-card pocket)

Notions: 2 yd. #5 tooth-type zipper tape

two #5 zipper pulls

one 9" zipper (dress or #2.5 tape with pull)

2⅝ yd. of 1½" medium-weight webbing

Optional: 1¾ yd. more webbing (for shoulder strap)

21" piece of ½" hook-and-loop tape

¾ yd. of ¾" twill tape

Optional: 5½ yd. more of ¾" twill tape (to clean-finish seam allowances)

Optional: one shoulder pad (for webbing; see "Glossary"), two snaphooks (swivel or plain), two web- or D-rings, and one slider—all 1½" (for shoulder strap)

1. Prepare fabric

Cut fabric as indicated on diagram, page 80. (*Tip:* As you cut the pieces, mark them to indicate what they are; this will make assembly easier and more goofproof. Write directly on the backs of each piece with a chalk pencil, or use masking or drafting tape.)

cut fabric:

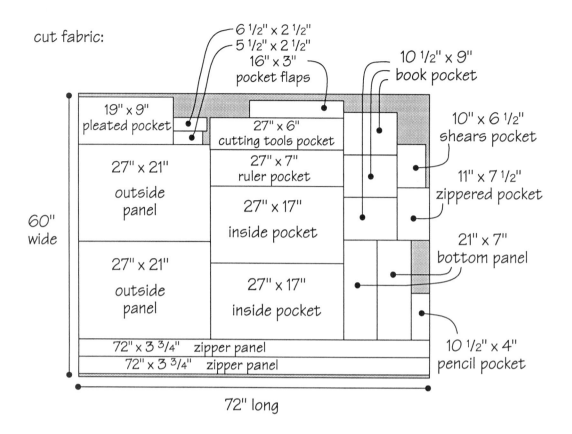

6 1/2" x 2 1/2"
5 1/2" x 2 1/2"
16" x 3"
pocket flaps

10 1/2" x 9"
book pocket

19" x 9"
pleated pocket

27" x 6"
cutting tools pocket

10" x 6 1/2"
shears pocket

27" x 21"

outside
panel

27" x 7"
ruler pocket

11" x 7 1/2"
zippered pocket

27" x 17"
inside pocket

60"
wide

27" x 21"

outside
panel

21" x 7"
bottom panel

27" x 17"

inside pocket

10 1/2" x 4"
pencil pocket

72" x 3 3/4"   zipper panel
72" x 3 3/4"   zipper panel

72" long

2. Make handles

a. Cut webbing into four pieces: two 27", and two 20". *Optional:* Sear ends.

b. Fold 20" pieces in half lengthwise; edgestitch, beginning and ending 4½" from ends, to make handles.

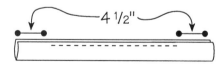

4 1/2"

c. Open out unstitched ends. Stitch flattened ends to outside panels, 9"

from side edges, and 3¾" down from top edge, angling them in slightly.

3 3/4"

9"

d. Edgestitch remaining pieces of webbing 4" from top edge, covering ends of handles.

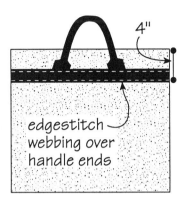

e. *Optional:* Stitch a 2¾" × 4" piece of clear vinyl to one outside panel, centered just below webbing, to hold a business card. (*Tip:* Place a piece of waxed or tissue paper between vinyl and presser foot while stitching, to keep it from sticking; tear off when through.)

3. Hem pockets

a. *Optional:* Serge or zigzag raw edges before turning under and stitching as follows.

b. Turn *one* long edge under ½" and topstitch:
- both inside pockets (27" × 17")
- ruler pocket (27" × 7")
- cutting tools pocket (27" × 6")
- shears pocket (10" × 6½")
- three book pockets (10½" × 9")
- pleated pocket (19" × 9")

c. Turn *both* long edges under ½" and topstitch:
- pencil pocket (10½" × 4")

4. Assemble one inside pocket

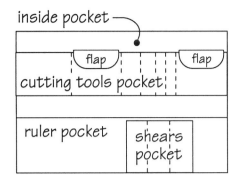

a. Turn under 6½" sides of shears pocket ½"; finger press. Edgestitch sides to ruler pocket, right sides up, 6" from right side edge, matching bottom edges. Mark two lines, 3" in from each side; stitch through all layers.

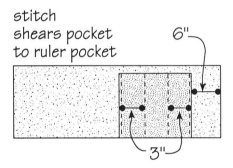

b. Baste ruler pocket to one inside pocket, right sides up, matching raw edges at bottom and sides.

c. Cut a 4" and a 3" piece of hook-and-loop tape. Stitch loop side of 4" piece to right side of cutting tools pocket, just below hem, 8" from left edge. Stitch 3" piece 1½" from right edge.

d. Turn under bottom edge of cutting tools pocket ½"; finger-press. Edgestitch along bottom to inside pocket, right sides up, 2" above ruler pocket, matching side edges. Baste sides together.

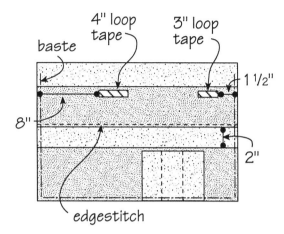

e. Make pocket flaps from 6½" × 2½" and 5½" × 2½" pieces of fabric: gently curve two bottom corners; turn under ¼" on sides and bottom; topstitch and edgestitch. (*Tip:* Trace around the rim of a juice glass to define curves.)

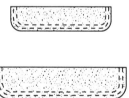

f. Stitch hook side of hook-and-loop tape to wrong side of pocket flaps, centered just above hem, 3" piece on small pocket and 4" piece on larger pocket.

g. Attach flaps to panel with hook-and-loop tape. Mark and stitch as follows:

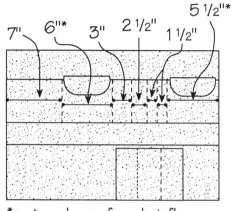

*or to edges of pocket flap

h. Fold under top raw edges of flaps, tucking them into pockets until fold is about ¼" above top edge of pocket; edgestitch to secure.

5. Assemble other inside pocket

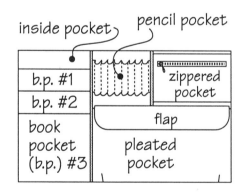

a. Position one book pocket on remaining inside pocket, right sides up, 5" from bottom edge, left raw edges aligned; stitch across bottom. Repeat

---

for second book pocket, positioning it on top of first and 2½" from bottom edge. Repeat for third book pocket, aligning bottom raw edges. Baste sides to inside pocket, using a ¼" seam allowance.

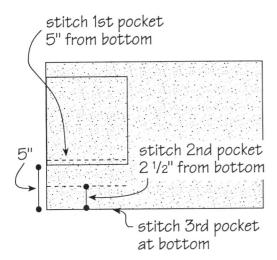

stitch 1st pocket 5" from bottom

5"

stitch 2nd pocket 2 1/2" from bottom

stitch 3rd pocket at bottom

b. Insert zipper into zipper pocket panel, centered 1½" down from top edge, using window-type construction method: draw a ½" × 9" rectangle at placement mark; cut down the middle to within ¼" of ends; clip to each corner; finger-press raw edges under; center zipper under opening; edgestitch in place.

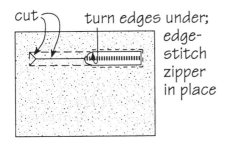

cut

turn edges under; edge-stitch zipper in place

c. Turn top and bottom edges of zipper pocket under ½"; finger-press. Position on inside pocket, right sides up, ½" from top edge, right raw edges aligned. Edgestitch along top and bottom. Baste sides, using a ½" seam allowance.

d. Mark inside pocket between book and zipper pockets as follows:

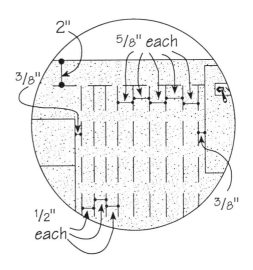

2"

5/8" each

3/8"

1/2" each

3/8"

e. Mark pencil pocket as follows:

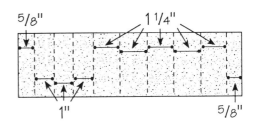

5/8"

1 1/4"

1"

5/8"

f. Stitch pencil pocket to inside pocket, aligning markings, right sides up. (*Tip:* Use a zipper foot and work from one side to the other.) (*Note:* Raw side edges will overlap book and zipper pockets ¼".)

---

g. Cut a 9" piece of twill tape; turn under and stitch one end. Center tape over seam allowances between pencil and zipper pockets, wrapping finished end over hem of inside pocket about ¾"; edgestitch.

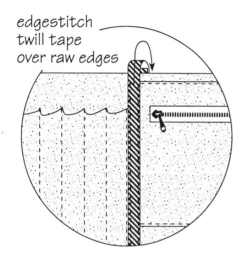

edgestitch
twill tape
over raw edges

h. Make pocket flap from 16" × 3" piece of fabric, as in Step 4e. Stitch loop side of 14" piece of hook-and-loop tape to wrong side, centered just above hem.

i. Stitch loop side of 14" piece of hook-and-loop tape to pleated pocket, cen-

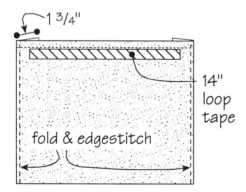

1 3/4"

14"
loop
tape

fold & edgestitch

tered just below hem. Fold pocket 1¾" from each side, wrong sides together; edgestitch along folds.

j. Baste sides (but not bottom) of pleated pocket to inside pocket using a ¼" seam allowance, right sides up, matching right and bottom raw edges, overlapping book pockets ¼". Edgestitch 18" piece of twill tape over seam allowances between pockets, as in Step 5g.

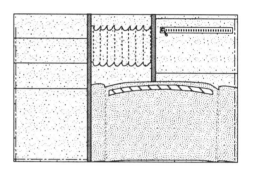

k. Position pocket flap on inside pocket, right sides together, ¾" from right edge, top edge of flap just touching hem of pleated pocket. Stitch ⅛" from raw edge of flap; stitch again ¼" from edge.

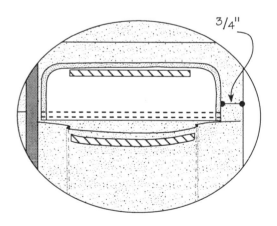

3/4"

Plate 5

Clockwise from top:
Huge Quilted Duffel (p. 62)
Library Book Bag, in denim
  (p. 72)

Coordinating
  Trimmed
  Pillowcase
  (p. 117)
Sleep-Over Bag
  (p. 112)
Quilter's
  Carryall, in
  Cordura
  (p. 78)

Plate 6

Clockwise from top:

Leather String Duffel, in
    cotton and Fabu-Leather
    (p. 61)
Travel Organizer, in
    Ultrasuede (p. 77)
Library Book Bag, in
    tapestry with Ultrasuede
    trim (p. 77)
Classic Open Tote (p. 32)
Victorian Carpetbag (p. 48)

Plate 7

Clockwise from top left:

Hosiery Roll-Up, in Ultrasuede Light,
  shown open and rolled (p. 108)
Lingerie Bag, in lace (p. 11)
Pocketed Jewelry Pouch, in Ultrasuede
  Light, shown cinched and open (p. 104)

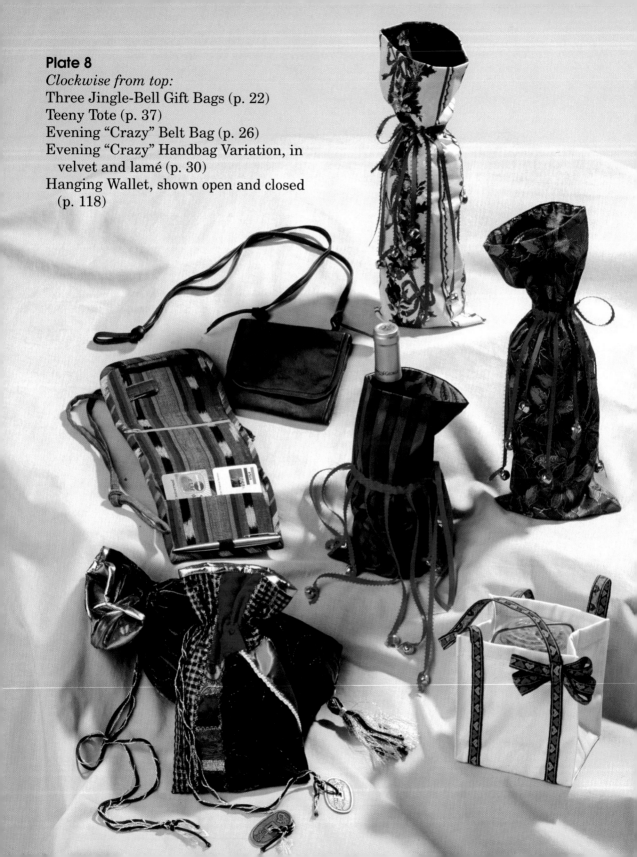

Plate 8

Clockwise from top:

Three Jingle-Bell Gift Bags (p. 22)
Teeny Tote (p. 37)
Evening "Crazy" Belt Bag (p. 26)
Evening "Crazy" Handbag Variation, in
  velvet and lamé (p. 30)
Hanging Wallet, shown open and closed
  (p. 118)

l. Baste pleated pocket to inside pocket at bottom, pleating equally at edge-stitching to lay flat, using a ¼" seam allowance.

6. Assemble side panels

a. Stitch one side of zipper tape to one zipper panel, right sides together, ¼" from zipper teeth. Turn right side out; finger-press seam allowances away from zipper teeth; edgestitch. Repeat for remaining half of zipper tape.

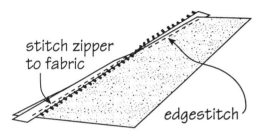

stitch zipper to fabric

edgestitch

b. Slide one zipper pull onto zipper tape; slide remaining zipper pull onto tape from opposite end; zip both pulls to center. (*Tip:* Zip zipper almost completely closed with first pull—to within 1" of end of tape—then slide the other pull on, to ensure that they meet evenly in the center.) Trim zipper strip to 71" long and 7" wide if necessary.

c. Place bottom panels right sides together; slip zipper panel between the two, matching raw edges; stitch across short end, through all layers, using a ½" seam allowance. (*Tip:* Remove zipper teeth from seam allowance area before stitching, by crushing and pulling off with pliers; stitch back and forth next to teeth to create a zipper stop.)

d. Stitch other end of zipper panel between bottoms in same manner. (*Tip:*

Fold and stack zipper panel until it's the same length as bottom panels, for easiest and most accurate stitching.)

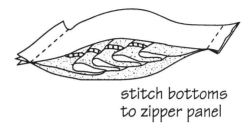

stitch bottoms
to zipper panel

e. Turn strip right side out. (*Note:* You should now have a 90" circle of fabric; adjust if necessary.) Edgestitch seamlines at bottom panel, through all layers.

f. Mark both edges of zipper panel 2¾" from bottom seamlines, and 19½" beyond that (these are corners). At each corner, clip seam allowance ⅜"; clip again ¼" and ½" on either side of each mark.

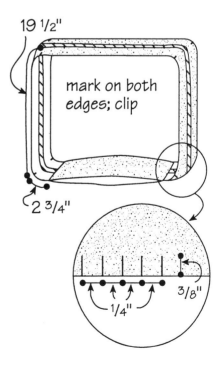

19 ½"

mark on both
edges; clip

2 ¾"

¼"   ⅜"

7. Finish bag

a. Baste one outside panel to one inside pocket, wrong sides together, using a scant ½" seam allowance. (*Note:* Be sure inside pockets are facing up, toward handle.) Repeat for remaining outside/inside panels.

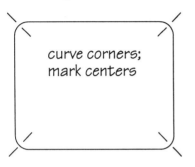

curve corners;
mark centers

b. Curve all corners. (*Tip:* Trace around the rim of a juice glass to define curves.) Mark the centers of each corner.

c. Pin one panel to zipper strip, right sides together, matching raw edges and corner markings, using a ½" seam allowance; stitch. Stitch again, 1/16" inside first stitching line, to reinforce. (*Tip:* Use a zipper foot to stitch the corners smoothly and easily.) Stitch remaining panel to other side of zipper strip in same manner.

d. *Optional:* Trim seam allowance to ⅜". Bind seam allowance with twill tape to finish raw edges.

Options, Ideas & Variations...

1 Customize the pockets to fit your particular tools and supplies.

2 Make a smaller, narrower bag, and you've got a small-quilt tote . . . or a briefcase . . . or a sewing/needle-work carryall—the possibilities are endless.

3 Add an adjustable shoulder strap. You'll need an additional 1¾ yards of webbing, plus hardware (see supply list, page 79).

a. Complete construction through Step 6e.

b. Cut two 4½" pieces of webbing; sear ends if desired. Loop webbing through web- or D-rings, enclosing one raw end within fold at other end.

loop
webbing
thru
D-ring

c. Position one loop of webbing on zipper panel, right sides up, ½" to the left of zipper tape, and 18¾" above bottom-panel seamline. Stitch through webbing to secure. Stitch remaining loop of webbing to opposite side of zipper panel in same manner.

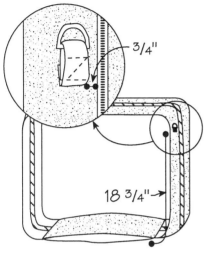

3/4"

18 3/4"

d. Continue with Step 6f, to end.

e. Make shoulder strap as instructed in Project 13, Step 8 (page 69).

4 Make one without the customized inside pockets—but smaller and wider—for a convenient soft-sided carry-on suitcase.

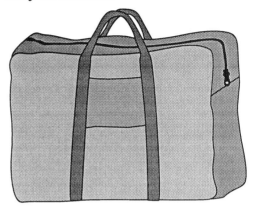

5 Make a large, thin bag to hold a child's portfolio of artful "masterpieces."

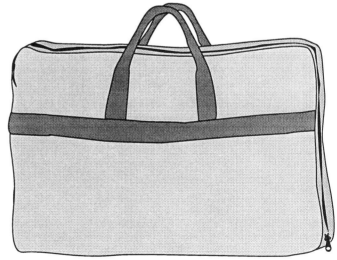

Project 16

Travel Organizer

This small shoulder bag is an ideal organizer for travel essentials—things like tickets, passport, itinerary, daily planner, receipts, credit cards and driver's license, a paperback book, sunglasses, a camera and film, a hand-held computer—anything you want to keep close at hand en route. It also makes a great gadget bag for things like cellular phones, camera gear, and binoculars. Its simple lines make it suitable for both men and women.

You can make it out of almost any medium-to heavyweight fabric, but a few notables jump quickly to mind: Ultrasuede and Fabu-Leather are soft and easy, elegant and fashionable;

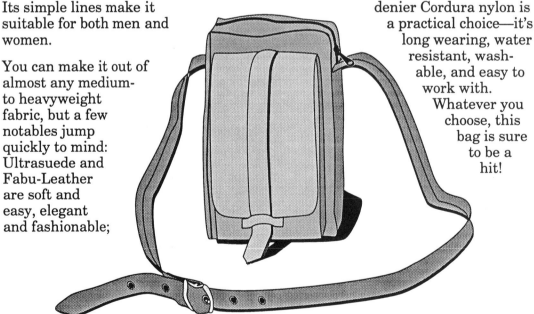

the drawback is that they do not wear particularly well or long, so they're best chosen for a fashionable rather than a durable accessory. Real leather is a classic choice—one that will stand the test of time—and perfect for a man's bag, although it's a bit finicky in the handling and not washable. (See "Sewing with Leather," page 55, for tips on choosing and sewing leather.) And 1,000-denier Cordura nylon is a practical choice—it's long wearing, water resistant, washable, and easy to work with. Whatever you choose, this bag is sure to be a hit!

How to Make a Travel Organizer

You'll Need (for one 9"×6"×3¼" bag)

Fabric: ¾ yd. of fabric (at least 45" wide), such as Cordura, denim, canvas, Ultrasuede, or leather

Notions: one 7" zipper

one 10" zipper

one ¾" buckle

Optional: 5 eyelets to fit buckle

1. Prepare fabric

Cut fabric as follows (also indicated on diagram, page 90):

- two 7"×10" (front and inside back)
- one 7"×2" (top back)
- one 7"×9" (bottom back)
- one 7"×8" (inside front pocket)
- one 5½"×7" (back pocket)
- one 7¾"×9" (front pocket)
- two 6"×7½" (pocket flaps)
- one 4½"×2½" (credit-card pocket)
- one 2½"×1" (loop)
- one 11½"×2½" (pocket strap)
- two 11"×2" (top zipper panel)
- one 21"×3½" (sides/bottom)
- one 45"×2¾" (shoulder strap)
- one 14"×2¾" (more shoulder strap)

Note: These measurements are for fabrics that do not ravel. If you choose

one that does, add ¼" to tops of all pocket pieces, flaps, and loop.

Tip: As you cut the pieces, mark them to indicate what they are; this will make assembly easier and more goof-proof. Write directly on the backs of each piece with a chalk pencil or use masking or drafting tape.

2. Assemble front panel

a. Stitch pocket flaps right sides together, using ½" seam allowance, leaving one short side open and rounding corners. Trim seam allowance to a scant ¼", notching curves. (*Tip:* Use pinking shears to trim and notch in one step.) Turn right side out; edgestitch.

Note: If fabric ravels, stitch around all four sides, leaving a 3" opening in top edge for turning.

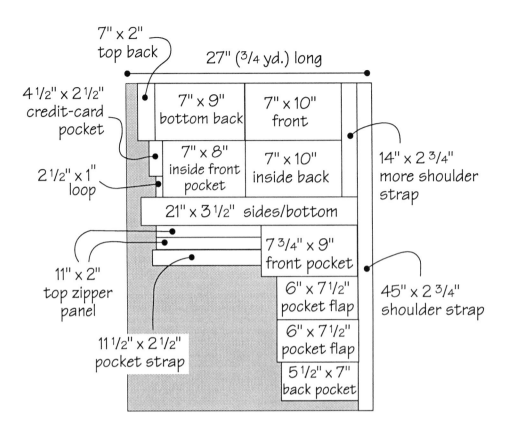

7" x 2" top back

27" (3/4 yd.) long

4 1/2" x 2 1/2" credit-card pocket

7" x 9" bottom back

7" x 10" front

7" x 8" inside front pocket

7" x 10" inside back

14" x 2 3/4" more shoulder strap

2 1/2" x 1" loop

21" x 3 1/2" sides/bottom

7 3/4" x 9" front pocket

11" x 2" top zipper panel

6" x 7 1/2" pocket flap

45" x 2 3/4" shoulder strap

11 1/2" x 2 1/2" pocket strap

6" x 7 1/2" pocket flap

5 1/2" x 7" back pocket

b. Fold pocket strap in half lengthwise, right sides together. Stitch, using ⅜" seam allowance. Finger-press seam allowance open. Position seam centered on one side of strap; stitch a point at one end; trim close to stitching. Turn right side out; edgestitch. Baste to pocket flap at center top.

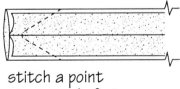

stitch a point
at one end of strap

c. Fold loop into thirds lengthwise (along the long edge); edgestitch. Position 6" from top edge of front pocket, centered. Turn ends under ¼"; stitch in place.

Note: If fabric ravels, fold under exposed raw edge ¼" before edgestitching.

d. Turn under ¼" on one long edge of credit-card pocket; topstitch. Turn under side and bottom edges ¼"; edgestitch to front pocket, centered 1¼" below top edge.

Note: If fabric ravels, turn under twice.

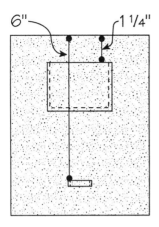

6"　1 ¼"

e. Turn under ½" on top edge of front pocket; topstitch.

Note: If fabric ravels, turn under ¼" first.

f. Trim 1¼" squares from bottom corners of front pocket.

trim bottom corners from pocket

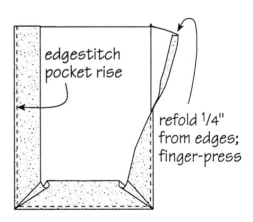

1 ¼"

1 ¼"

g. Fold diagonally at one corner, right sides together, meeting raw edges of cutout. Stitch, using ¼" seam allowance. Repeat for other cutout

corner. Finger-press seam allowances open; turn pocket right side out.

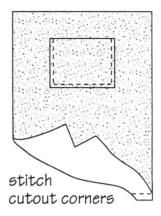

stitch cutout corners

h. Fold pocket flat, along lines defined by stitched-in corner points; edgestitch. Unfold and refold ¼" from side and bottom edges; finger-press.

edgestitch pocket rise

refold ¼" from edges; finger-press

i. Mark pocket placement on front, 1" from sides and bottom edges. Position pocket on front just inside placement marks; edgestitch along fold at pocket sides and bottom.

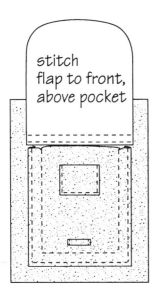

edgestitch
pocket to front

1"

1"

j. Place pocket flap upside down on front, right sides together, butting top edge of flap to top edge of pocket. Stitch ¼" from edge of fabric; stitch again right next to edge to reinforce.

stitch
flap to front,
above pocket

k. Turn under ½" on top edge of inside front pocket; topstitch. Baste to front,

wrong sides together, matching side and bottom edges.

Note: If fabric ravels, turn under ¼" first.

3. Assemble back panel

a. Position 7" zipper on bottom back, right sides together, with zipper pull ¾" from end; stitch ⅛" from zipper teeth. Stitch remaining side of zipper to top back in same manner. Finger-press seam allowances toward fabric; edgestitch. Measure length; trim fabric to 10" long if necessary.

b. Turn under ½" on top edge of back pocket; topstitch.

Note: If fabric ravels, turn under ¼" first.

c. Turn side edges of back pocket under ¼"; edgestitch to back, 1" from sides, bottom edges even.

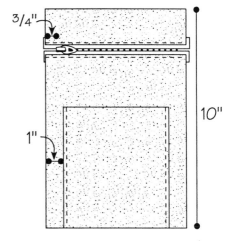

3/4"

1"

10"

d. Baste back to inside back, wrong sides together, around all four sides.

4. Complete zipper panel

a. Position 10" zipper on one top zipper panel, right sides together, with zipper pull ¾" from end; stitch about ⅛" from zipper teeth. Stitch remaining side of zipper to remaining top zipper panel in same manner. Finger-press seam allowances toward fabric; edgestitch. Trim fabric to 3½" wide if necessary.

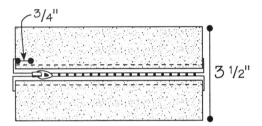

b. Fold both shoulder strap pieces in half lengthwise, right sides together; stitch, using ⅜" seam allowances. Finger-press seam allowances open. Position seams centered on one side of strap; stitch a point at one end of long handle and straight across at one end of short handle. Trim close to stitching. Turn right side out; edgestitch.

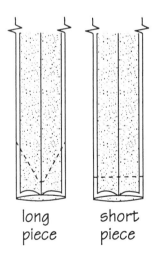

long piece   short piece

c. Baste one shoulder strap to each short edge of sides/bottom strip, centered, right sides together, matching raw edges.

d. Stitch zipper panel to sides/bottom strip along short edges, right sides together, using a ½" seam allowance. Finger-press seam allowances toward sides/bottom; edgestitch and topstitch.

e. Clip seam allowance a scant ½" on both sides of strip, 2" above seamline, and 7" below seamline (these are the corners).

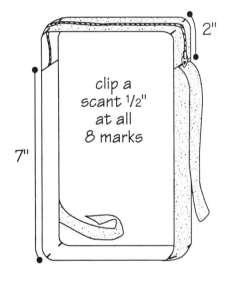

clip a scant ½" at all 8 marks

2"

7"

5. Finish bag

a. Pin sides/bottom and zipper strip to front panel, right sides together, zipper at top, turning corners at clips. Stitch, using a ½" seam allowance, barely catching fabric in stitching at corners.

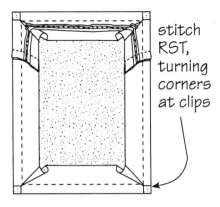

stitch
RST,
turning
corners
at clips

b. Trim seam allowance to a scant ¼"; trim out corners on front panel. Turn right side out. *Optional:* Edgestitch seamlines.

Note: If fabric ravels, clean-finish seam allowances before turning.

c. Open zipper a few inches. Repeat Steps 5a and 5b for back panel.

d. Attach buckle to end of short shoulder strap, according to manufacturer's directions. Make five holes in long shoulder strap, 1½" apart, beginning 6" from pointed end.

Optional: Finish raw edges of holes with eyelets, if desired.

Optional: Wrap a ¼"-wide and 3"-long tube of fabric around short shoulder strap, an inch or so below buckle; tack in place on back of strap. Tuck end of strap through loop after buckling.

5

Rolls & Pouches

This chapter is devoted to bags and
holders that either roll or draw up to
hold their contents—
two age-old forms.

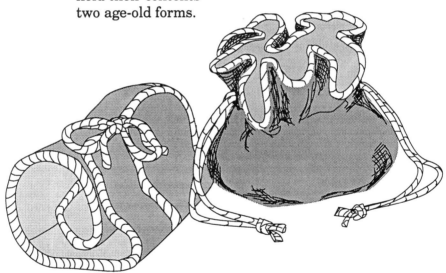

Project 17

Reversible Child's Play Mat

Difficulty: ✂

This mat provides a convenient way to transport loose, bulky toys such as cars and trucks, building blocks, small dolls and their furniture, or action figures and their accoutrements. The mat can be spread out flat to provide a clean and inviting playing surface almost anywhere.

And when you're done, cleanup is easy: just grab the drawstring and go. Choose a preprinted street, farm, or woodland fabric for the inside to add a scenic dimension to your child's play, or exercise your creativity and appliqué, embroider, or paint an imaginative environment that's all your own.

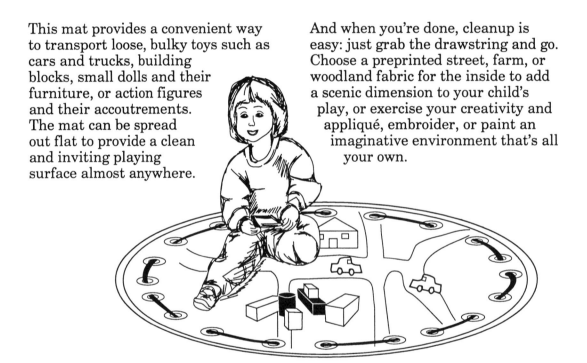

How to Make a Reversible Child's Play Mat

1. Cut fabric

a. Cut a circle of print fabric 44" in diameter.

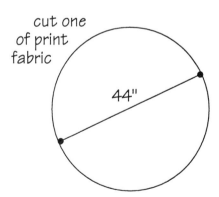

cut one of print fabric

44"

b. Place circle on solid fabric, wrong sides together. Pin frequently, close to edge. Cut through both layers, barely trimming edge of print fabric.

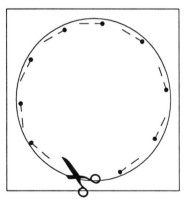

cut through both layers, barely trimming edge of print fabric

---

2. Mark and reinforce for grommets

a. Fold fabric into sixteenths; mark placement for grommets close to edge at each fold.

b. Fuse a scrap of interfacing between layers at each placement mark.

3. Bind raw edge

a. Serge or zigzag around raw edge to stabilize and secure.

b. Find the shorter side of bias tape.

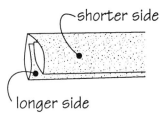

With shorter side toward edge of fabric, unfold end of tape; place right side down on fabric, matching raw edges.

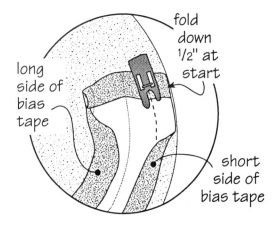

c. Turn down end of tape ½". Stitch exactly in fold line nearest raw edges, through all layers (unfolding tape as you go), all the way around.

d. Overlap and stitch bias tape about ¾" past beginning fold. Trim off excess.

e. Wrap bias tape snugly around raw edge of fabric. Stitch in the ditch; since the side of the bias tape you wrapped around the fabric is the slightly longer one, you will automatically catch and secure it with your stitching.

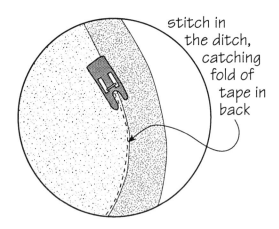

4. Finish bag

a. Install grommets at placement marks according to manufacturer's directions.

Note: If you don't have or don't want to invest in a grommet-setting tool—or if

---

Hold It!

you just hate setting grommets your-self—you can usually hire out the service. Check your yellow pages under "Boat Covers, Tops & Upholstery." Prices and available sizes vary, so call first; I found that most places in my area would set ⅜" grommets for 50¢ to $1 apiece.

b. Thread cording through grommets, beginning and ending on solid-fabric side of mat. Knot ends; trim excess.

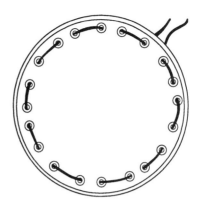

Options, Ideas & Variations...

1 Let your child help design and create the "environment." Even small children have definite ideas about what they like . . . not to mention a boundless imagination that may result in a delightful (or perhaps bizarre) combination of elements.

2 Make this bag out of a picnicky or beachy print, and you've got an easy bag plus sit-upon. For picnic use, consider lining it with an insulating fabric. If damp ground may be a problem, choose a waterproof fabric for the bottom.

Project 18

Donn's Tool Roll

Difficulty: ✂✂

One of my favorite people is Donn Fuller. He's not only gregarious, he's also a treat to know: generous to a fault, enthusiastic about new things, and eager to share what he knows—plus he sews. When I told Donn I was writing a bag book, he immediately forwarded a number of his own designs, among them, this wonderfully easy-to-make roll-up tool bag.

He designed it for toting an assortment of "regular" tools, like wrenches and pliers and screwdrivers. But you could scale it down to hold smaller tools, such as wrenches and tire-repair tools for your favorite bicyclist . . . or paintbrushes and palette knives for your favorite artist . . . or tent stakes and cooking utensils for your favorite camper . . . or—why not?—scissors, shears, a ruler, seam ripper, and other sewing tools for yourself.

How to Make Donn's Tool Roll

You'll Need (for a 16½"× 27" bag)

Fabric: ⅞ yd. of sturdy fabric, 60" wide, such as 1,000-denier Cordura (this is enough fabric for two bags)

Optional: 2¾"× 4" rectangle of clear vinyl (for business-card pocket)

Notions: 2¼ yd. of 1½" nylon or polypropylene webbing

two 1½" side-release buckles (also called parachute clips)

chalk or other marker; ruler

---

1. Prepare fabric
Cut fabric 30"× 30".

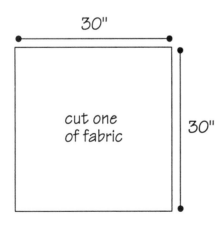

30"

30"

cut one
of fabric

2. Attach webbing
a. Cut webbing into three pieces: two 34" long (for straps) and one 13" long (for handle). Mark each strap 10" from one end. *Optional:* Sear ends to keep from raveling.

b. Thread buckle end of one side-release buckle onto one strap, up to marking. Fold and stitch webbing together just below buckle. Repeat for remaining buckle and strap.

10"

c. Turn under ½" at short end of each strap. Position straps on right side of fabric, 9½" from top and bottom edges and 7" from one side edge. Edgestitch, ending 3" from edge of fabric. Reinforce stitching on both sides of buckle. (*Tip:* Use a zipper foot to stitch close to buckle.)

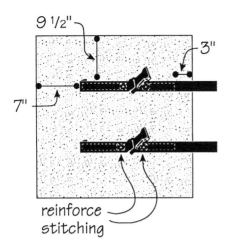

reinforce stitching

d. Mark center of handle (13" piece of webbing). Fold edges in, meeting them at center; stitch straight across. Taper folds out, ending 2½" on each side of center; edgestitch. Fold raw ends of handle under ½".

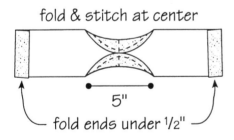

fold & stitch at center

5"

fold ends under ½"

e. Position handle flat over straps, 3" from edge of fabric. Stitch securely over straps.

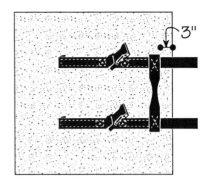

3. Make pockets

a. Fold under ¼" on top and bottom edges; topstitch. *Optional:* Serge or zigzag edges before folding.

b. Mark fabric as follows (or size to accommodate specific tools):

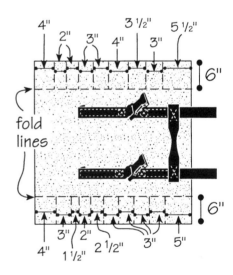

fold lines

c. Fold top and bottom edges toward center along marked fold lines. Stitch along markings, through both layers, to create pockets. Baste raw edges together.

fold

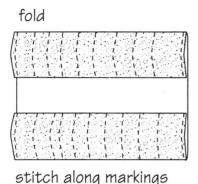

stitch along markings

4. Finish bag

a. Fold raw side edges to inside ½"; fold in again ⅝". Edgestitch.

b. *Optional:* Cut a 2¾" × 4" clear vinyl rectangle. Topstitch a scant ¼" around three sides, centered on front of bag

just beyond handle. (*Tip:* Place a scrap of waxed paper between vinyl and presser foot to keep from sticking; tear off when finished.) Insert business card through open end.

optional
calling-card pocket

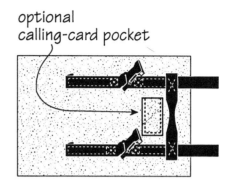

c. Thread prong ends of side-release buckles onto loose ends of webbing. Roll up bag and clip to close.

Options, Ideas & Variations...

stitch flap to inside
along folded edge

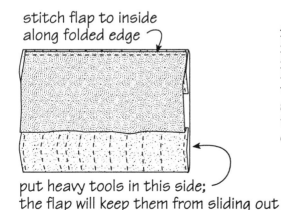

put heavy tools in this side;
the flap will keep them from sliding out

Add a security flap (or two). Large, heavy tools—particularly ones that have a skewed center of balance, like hammers—may slide out of the bag when you carry it. To prevent this, stitch a piece of fabric to the inside of the bag along the folded edge after completing Step 4b. (For this bag, cut fabric for each flap to 28" × 12".
  Clean-finish all edges—turn under twice, ¼" each time, and stitch—before stitching flap to bag.)

Project 19

Pocketed Jewelry Pouch

Variations on this clever bag have been widely featured in gift shops and catalogs over the past couple of years, and for good reason. It's as pretty as it is practical. Ask anyone who has one: they wouldn't be without it to keep earrings, bracelets, and necklaces safe and separate when they travel. It is easy and quick to make and takes just a bit of fabric—perfect for gift giving. Make it out of lightweight synthetic suede with a satin lining and decorative piping for an absolutely elegant gift, for yourself or for a special friend. And for the truly deserving, make a Hosiery Roll-Up to match (see Project #20).

How to Make a Pocketed Jewelry Pouch

1. Prepare fabric

Cut one 15" and one 11" circle from both the suede and satin fabrics.

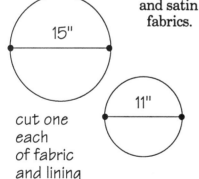

cut one each of fabric and lining

2. Make buttonholes (for cording)

a. Fold large (15") suede circle in half, wrong sides together. Mark placement for ½" buttonholes on fold, beginning 1⅝" and ending 2⅛" from each end.

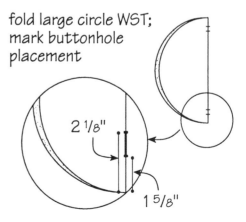

fold large circle WST; mark buttonhole placement

2 ⅛"

1 ⅝"

b. Fuse scraps of lightweight fusible interfacing to wrong side of suede fabric under buttonhole placement marks, according to manufacturer's directions. (*Tip:* Test first on fabric scraps.)

c. Stitch a narrow rectangle, ½" long, at each buttonhole placement mark, using a short stitch length. Slit fabric within rectangles.

3. Finish circles

a. Baste piping to right side of large suede circle, stitching next to cording, ½" from edge of fabric.

b. Pin large satin circle to large suede circle, right sides together. Stitch just inside basting stitches, leaving 3" open for turning. Repeat for small circles, using ½" seam allowance. Trim and clip seam allowances close to stitching. (*Tip:* Use pinking shears to trim and clip in one step.)

c. Turn circles right side out. Slipstitch openings closed. Edgestitch around small circle.

d. Mark and stitch casing on suede side of large circle, 1" and 1¾" from edge of

fabric. (*Note:* Buttonholes should fall between stitching lines.) (*Tip:* Use a walking, or dual-feed, foot for pucker-free stitching.)

4. Stitch circles together

a. Mark smaller circle into eighths, on right side of suede fabric. (*Tip:* Fold into eighths and mark along folds; or, if you have a gridded ironing board cover or cutting mat, use the horizontal, vertical, and bias lines as a guide for marking.) Mark a 3" circle in center.

b. Place smaller circle centered on larger circle, satin sides together. Pin along markings. Stitch along markings, through all layers.

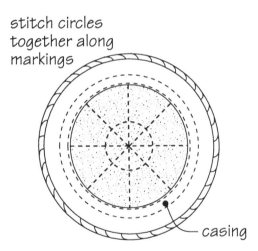

stitch circles together along markings

casing

5. Finish bag

a. Cut decorative cording in half. Thread one piece through casing, beginning and ending at one button-hole. Knot ends together.

b. Thread remaining piece of cording through casing, beginning and ending at opposite buttonhole. Knot ends together.

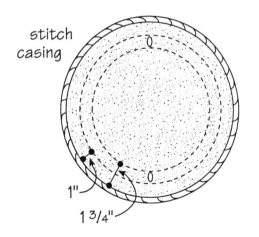

stitch casing

1"

1 ¾"

Hold It!

thread cording thru
buttonhole; knot ends

c. Pull knotted ends of cording in
opposite directions to cinch.

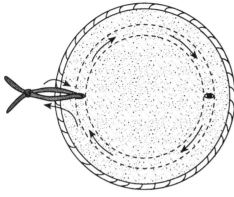

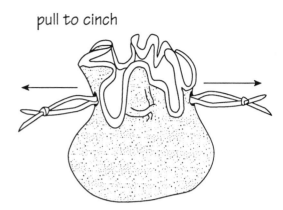

pull to cinch

repeat for other side

Options, Ideas & Variations...

1 Omit the piping to simplify construction; edgestitch the larger circle instead. Or even quicker, decoratively serge the edges.

2 To keep jewelry from tarnishing, use an antitarnish fabric instead of satin as a lining, such as Atlantic Anti-Tarnish Cloth or Pacific Silver-Cloth (if not available in your fabric store, see "Sources and Resources" section for mail-order vendors).

3 Make the bag out of a glitzy evening fabric, increase the size a bit, and carry it as an elegant little purse. Consider layering lace or mesh fabric over a base fabric, and then stitching on some beads or findings for some extra sizzle.

4 Different-size pocketed pouches might come in handy for a number of uses, for instance, for picnicking or for storing things like toys and makeup.

Project 20

Hosiery Roll-Up

Difficulty: ✂✂

I'm not easy on stockings. If I stuff them into a suitcase, inevitably, I catch them in the zipper. And Baggies are so déclassé. So I've always wanted something to keep my precious run-free pairs protected—hence, this bag.

Make it out of Ultrasuede Light and line it with satin to match the Pocketed Jewelry Pouch (Project #19) for a truly elegant ensemble, either for gift giving or for yourself. The yardage given for the Pocketed Jewelry Pouch is sufficient to make both bags.

How to Make a Hosiery Roll-Up

You'll Need (for one 6"×14" bag, when open)

Fabric: 7"×15" panel of fabric, such as Ultrasuede or Ultrasuede Light (can use leftovers from the Pocketed Jewelry Pouch, Project #19)

        ½ yd. smooth lining fabric, such as satin (do not use flannel-backed satin; it's too thick)

Notions: 1¼ yd. decorative corded piping

        ¾ yd. of ⅛" to ¼" decorative cording, to match piping, or ⅛" to ¼" ribbon

1. Prepare fabric

a. Cut one 7"×15" panel of suede fabric.

b. Cut rectangles from lining fabric:
- one 7"×15"
- three 7"×11"
- one 7"×10"

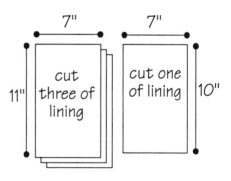

c. Curve corners on both 7"×15" panels, and on the 7"×10" panel. (*Tip:* Use a juice glass to define curves.)

---

2. Attach pockets to lining

a. Fold three 7" × 11" lining panels in half crosswise. Stitch or serge, using ½" seam allowances. Turn right sides out. Press flat, with seam at bottom.

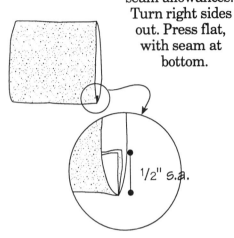

1/2" s.a.

b. Press 7" × 10" panel in half crosswise, wrong sides together.

c. Place one of the three seamed pockets on right side of lining panel, 4" from top. Edgestitch along bottom.

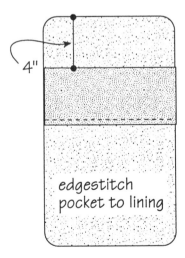

4"

edgestitch
pocket to lining

d. Place another of the three seamed pockets on right side of lining panel, 2" below top of previous pocket. Edgestitch along bottom.

e. Repeat for remaining pockets, ending with unseamed pocket aligned with bottom edges of lining panel.

f. Baste pockets to lining along sides.

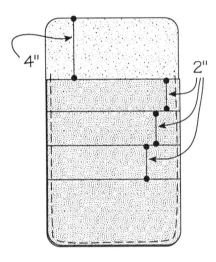

4"

2"

3. Assemble bag

a. Baste piping to fabric, right sides together, raw edges toward edge of fabric, stitching close to cording, ½" from fabric edges.

b. Pin lining unit to fabric, right sides together. Stitch from wrong side of fabric, just inside basting stitches, leaving a 3" opening on one side for turning. (*Tip:* Use a zipper foot.) Trim seam allowances to ¼".

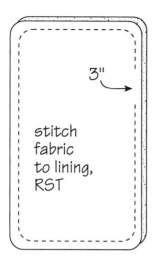

3"

stitch
fabric
to lining,
RST

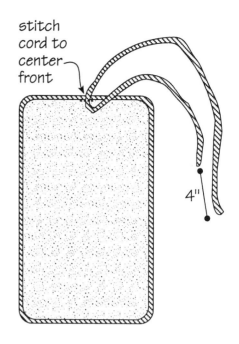

stitch
cord to
center
front

4"

c. Turn right side out. Slipstitch opening shut.

4. Finish bag

a. Fold cord so ends are offset about 4"; stitch to center front edge through fold.

b. Roll up bag, wrap ends of cord around it in opposite directions, and tie closed.

---

*Chapter 5: **Rolls & Pouches***

Project 21

Sleep-Over Bag

This is not the bag for winter camping in the Minnesota Boundary Waters area, but it really fills the bill for a slumber party or for warm- to cool-weather overnights: it's easy to roll, lightweight, and just plain fun. Pair it with the Huge Quilted Duffel (Project #13) for a great combo, and add a coordinating pillowcase to complete the ensemble (see box, page 117, for directions). To ward off the chill of cool nights, choose a soft and cozy flannel for the lining; for sultry summer days, select a lightweight cotton instead.

Hold the layers together with simple bar tacks, or finish the bag with a flourish of freehand quilting (see box, page 65, for tips on freehand machine quilting).

The following instructions are for a Sleep-Over Bag that will fit most kids between the ages of seven and ten; you may want to adjust the size if your sleeper is a lot bigger or smaller. Use the entire width of your fabric, whether it's 54", 60", or somewhere in between (that's why measurements are given in "abouts" and "approximatelys").

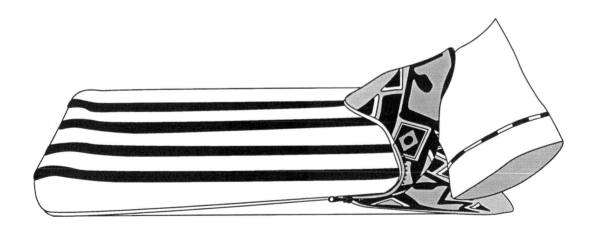

How to Make a Sleep-Over Bag

You'll Need (for one approximately 60" × 28" bag)

Fabric: 1¾ yd. each of inner and outer fabric, at least 54" wide, preferably 60" wide (or 3½ yd. of each for 36"- and 45"-wide fabrics)

             Optional: ¾ yd. additional or contrast fabric (for welting)

             medium- to high-loft polyester batting, about 62" × 65" ("twin" is the closest packaged size)

Notions: 5½ yd. of ½" welting (or 5½ yd. of ½" cording and extra fabric to make your own; see above for yardage)

             1½ yd. of #5 zipper tape, and one zipper pull

             2 yd. of 1" webbing

             two 1" side-release buckles (also called parachute clips)

             several dozen safety pins

1. Prepare fabric

a. Trim inner and outer fabrics to same size, squaring raw edges; each will be approximately 60" wide by 63" long. (*Note:* For 36"- and 45"-width fabrics, piece inner and outer fabrics to about 60" × 63" before trimming.)

b. Trim 1" off width of inner fabric (to allow for turn of the cloth). Gently curve two top corners on both fabrics.

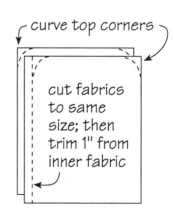

curve top corners

cut fabrics to same size; then trim 1" from inner fabric

2. Apply welting

a. *Optional:* Make your own welting.

b. Pin welting to right side of outer fabric, raw edges even, along side and top edges. Baste close to cording.

baste welting to outer fabric

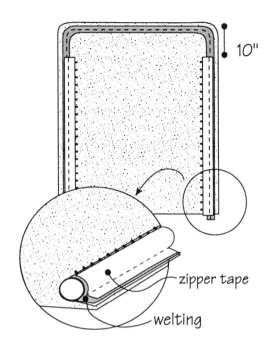

10"

zipper tape

welting

3. Insert zipper

a. Separate zipper tape. Stitch a folded scrap of fabric to one end of each zipper tape half, to create a secure stop at top of zipper.

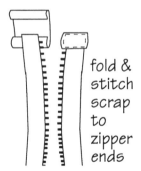

fold & stitch scrap to zipper ends

b. Baste one zipper tape half to one of the sides, over welting basting stitches, about ⅛" from edge of zipper tape, positioning zipper stop 10" from top edge of fabric. Repeat for other side.

4. Stitch bag

a. Place batt on flat surface; smooth with hands. Place inner fabric on top, right side up, with batting extending at least 1" all around; smooth with hands. Place outer fabric on top of inner fabric, right sides together. Pin all three layers together around sides and top, matching fabric raw edges. Rough-cut batting to extend about 1" beyond fabric edges if necessary.

b. Stitch layers together around three pinned sides, as close to cording as possible, easing outer fabric to fit. (*Tip:* Stitch with batting layer next to feed dogs, and wrong side of outer fabric under presser foot; use a zipper foot and stitch just inside basting stitches.) Ease as much excess outer fabric as possible toward the center of the top seam, where the bag will fold.

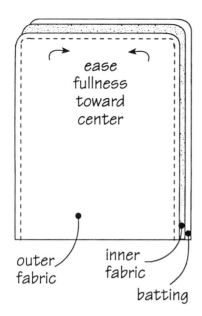

ease
fullness
toward
center

outer
fabric

inner
fabric

batting

c. Turn bag right side out. Smooth. Pin layers together with safety pins every 10" or less. Machine quilt or bar tack every 6" to 8" to hold layers together. *Optional:* Mark quilting design or placement for bar tacks on outer fabric after pinning.

To machine quilt: See box, page 65.

To bar tack: Lower or cover feed dogs; stitch in place ("zero" stitch-width setting) three to four times; next, widen stitch and tack four to five times; finish by stitching in place several times again to lock. Trim threads.

d. Fold bag in half, right sides out. Install zipper pull onto tape; zip closed. *Optional:* Remove zipper teeth from bottom ¾" of tape, using pliers.

e. Make an enclosed bottom seam: Stitch across bottom, through all

layers, about ½" from edge of fabrics. (*Tip:* Position fold slightly off-center, so that zipper and welting fall entirely on one side of bag.) Trim seam allowance to ⅜".

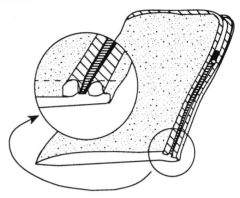

f. Turn bag inside out. Stitch bottom seam again, about ¾" from fold to enclose raw edges. Turn right side out.

5. Finish bag

a. Cut webbing into two equal pieces; clean-finish ends (sear nylon and polypropylene; stitch cotton and blends).

b. Stitch buckle part of side-release buckles to one end of each piece of webbing.

c. Fold bag in half lengthwise. Mark positions for two pieces of webbing at bottom of bag, about 3" from each side.

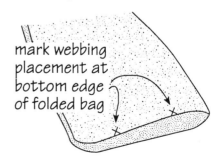

mark webbing placement at bottom edge of folded bag

---

d. Unfold bag. Stitch webbing to bag at marks, through top layer and seam allowance, with buckles hanging over edge about 1".

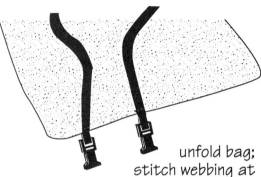

unfold bag;
stitch webbing at
placement marks, through all layers

e. Thread prong-end of side-release buckles onto other ends of webbing.

6. Roll up bag

Fold bag in half lengthwise. Roll up tightly, beginning from top of bag. Wrap webbing around rolled bag; clip buckles shut. Pull ends of webbing to cinch tight.

Optional: Trim excess webbing; clean-finish ends.

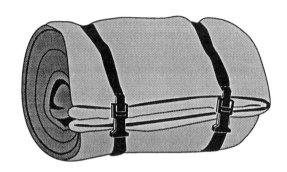

Options, Ideas & Variations...

1 Skip the welting; it's faster and easier.

2 Change the length and width. Make a teensy-weensy one for dolls or teddys; they're a real hit for kids' birthday gifts.

3 Shape the ends: either expand the bottom to accommodate a pillow or hollow out the neck (top) to accommodate the head.

Hold It!

How to Make a Coordinating Trimmed Pillowcase

Choose a solid cotton broadcloth (or some other fabric with identical right and wrong sides) to coordinate with your Sleep-Over Bag fabric. You'll need 1 yard of 44"-wide fabric, and 41" (about 1¼ yd.) of trim. Use a 1" bias strip of your Sleep-Over Bag fabric, folded in half lengthwise; or choose lace, corded piping, or even a ruffled trim.

- Cut the fabric to 35" × 40".

- Fold in half (to 35" × 20"). Serge or stitch across one 20" end, using a ⅜" seam allowance. Clean-finish edges, if stitched.

- Make a scant ⅜" clip through both side edges, 6" from unseamed end. Serge or stitch side seam, using a ⅜" seam allowance, ending at clip. Clean-finish edges, if stitched.

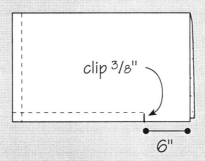

stitch bottom and side using 3/8" s.a.

clip 3/8"

6"

- Turn pillowcase right side out. Fold side seam allowances to right side above clip. Serge or stitch remaining 6" section of side seam.

- Fold down raw edge ½"; press. Turn down again 3"; press. Pin trim between pillowcase and hem edge; edgestitch through all layers.

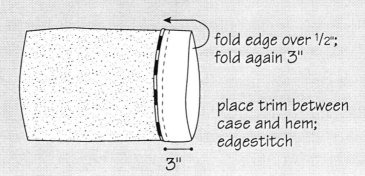

fold edge over 1/2"; fold again 3"

place trim between case and hem; edgestitch

3"

Project 22

Hanging Wallet

Difficulty: ✂✂✂✂

This "wallet-on-a-string" is the dressier cousin of the fanny pack (or "bum bag," as it is known in Europe)—just big enough for your essentials, it's light-weight and easy to wear. This one has the added convenience of a remov-able shoulder strap; just untie it, and slip the wallet into a purse. The instructions are for a wallet with two credit-card pockets, a miscellany pocket (closed with hook-and-loop tape), a zippered compartment for coins and currency, a side-opening pocket with a tab closure to hold other necessities (such as a notepad, shopping lists, and tissues), plus an elastic loop for a pen or pencil . . .

but you can easily customize it to suit your own needs, by changing pockets and/or fabrics. If you choose to make this bag from real or synthetic leather, be sure to read "Sewing with Leather," on page 55, before you begin.

How to Make a Hanging Wallet

You'll Need (for a finished 4½"×5½" bag)

Fabric: ¾ yd. fabric (*Note:* This is enough for two bags if pattern is not a concern. If you use a fabric with a definite pattern or nonrepeating stripe, you may want to buy at least 2 yd. and use a 7"-wide continuous length for the Hanging Wallet and the remaining fabric for a vest or another bag.)

½ yd. lining fabric

½ yd. medium- to heavyweight fusible interfacing

Notions: one 7" dress zipper

5¼" of ¾" hook-and-loop tape

1½" elastic (at least ¾" wide)

marking tool (such as chalk) and ruler

1. Prepare fabric

a. Cut the following from fabric (see diagram, page 120, for layout):

- 5½" × 12⅝" (outside)
- 5½" × 5" (inside top)
- 5½" × 8" (inside bottom)
- 5½" × 4¼" (miscellany pocket)
- 5½" × 3" (credit-card pocket)
- 70" × 1½" (shoulder strap/loop strip) *Note:* Piece by seaming diagonally (to reduce bulk).
- 3" × 2½" (tab)
- 37" × 1½" (bias binding strip) *Note:* Cut on bias.

Tip: As you cut the pieces, mark them to indicate what they are; this will make assembly easier and more goof-proof. Write directly on the backs of each piece with a chalk pencil, or use masking or drafting tape.

b. Cut the following from lining fabric:

- 5½" × 12⅝" (outside)
- 5½" × 5" (inside top)
- 5½" × 8" (inside bottom)
- 5½" × 4" (miscellany pocket)
- 5½" × 2¾" (credit-card pocket)

c. Cut the following from interfacing:

- 5⅜" × 12½" (outside)
- 5⅜" × 4⅞" (inside top)
- 5⅜" × 7⅞" (inside bottom)
- 2" × 1½" (tab)

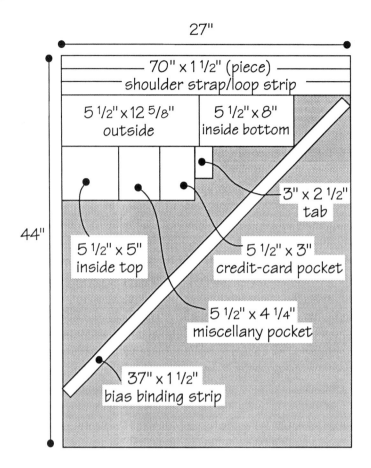

27"

70" x 1 1/2" (piece)
shoulder strap/loop strip

5 1/2" x 12 5/8"
outside

5 1/2" x 8"
inside bottom

44"

3" x 2 1/2"
tab

5 1/2" x 5"
inside top

5 1/2" x 3"
credit-card pocket

5 1/2" x 4 1/4"
miscellany pocket

37" x 1 1/2"
bias binding strip

d. Fuse interfacing to wrong side of corresponding fabric pieces, according to manufacturer's directions.

2. Assemble inside top

a. Draw a 2½" x ¼" window on wrong side of inside-top lining panel, 1" from side and ¾" from top edge. Place lining on inside-top fabric panel, right sides together. Pin. Stitch along marked lines, using short stitch length.

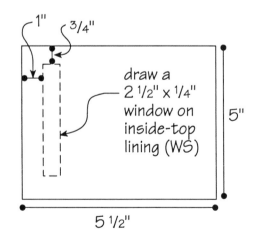

1"   3/4"

draw a
2 1/2" x 1/4"
window on
inside-top
lining (WS)

5"

5 1/2"

b. Cut down center and to corners of window. Turn right side out through opening; press. Edgestitch around window. Baste fabric and lining together close to raw edges.

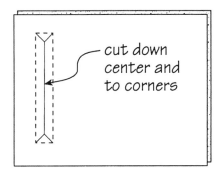

cut down center and to corners

c. Fold tab in half lengthwise. Stitch across one end and down side, using ½" seam allowance. Trim off corner of seam allowance.

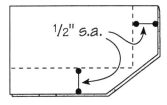

½" s.a.

d. Turn tab right side out; edgestitch. Cut ½" from hook-and-loop tape. Edgestitch loop side to finished end of tab, wrong sides together.

stitch loop side of hook-and-loop tape to wrong side of tab

e. Position hook side on right side of fabric, ⅜" from edge of opening, centered; edgestitch in place.

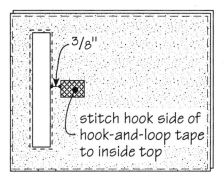

3/8"

stitch hook side of hook-and-loop tape to inside top

f. Adhere tab to inside top with hook-and-loop tape. Thread raw end of tab through opening, to wrong side; baste at side edge through all layers.

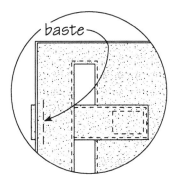

baste

3. Assemble inside bottom

a. Stitch lining to fabric at top edges of credit-card and miscellany pockets, right sides together, using ¼" seam allowance. Press seam allowances toward lining. Fold each pocket right sides out, matching raw edges; baste bottom edges together; press flat.

b. Cut remaining piece (4¾") of hook-and-loop tape in half lengthwise; set one half aside. Edgestitch loop side of remaining half to top edge of miscellany pocket, wrong sides together, ⅜" from each side of pocket.

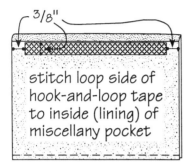

stitch loop side of
hook-and-loop tape
to inside (lining) of
miscellany pocket

c. Mark stitching line on credit-card pocket, 2¾" from either side. Position on top of miscellany pocket, fabric sides up, matching sides and bottom edges. Stitch along marked line.

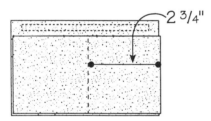

stitch credit-card to
miscellany pocket at center

d. Baste inside-bottom lining to corresponding fabric panel, close to raw edges. Mark a line 3⅝" from bottom, on right side of fabric. Position hook side of hook-and-loop tape centered on fabric, with top edge along marked line; edgestitch.

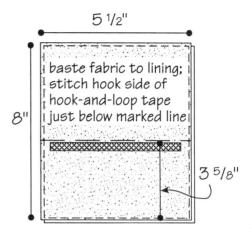

baste fabric to lining;
stitch hook side of
hook-and-loop tape
just below marked line

e. Position pocket unit at bottom of inside panel, matching hook-and-loop tape and raw edges. Fold elastic in half crosswise. Position at center bottom, matching raw edges. Baste pockets and elastic to panel close to raw edges.

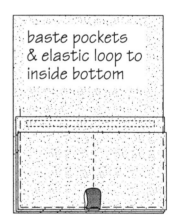

baste pockets
& elastic loop to
inside bottom

4. Insert zipper

a. Clean-finish top edge of inside-bottom unit, and bottom edge of inside-top.

b. Position zipper at lower edge of inside-top, right sides together, raw

---

edges aligned, with ends of zipper tape extending equally at both sides. Stitch close to zipper teeth, about ⅜" from edge of fabric.

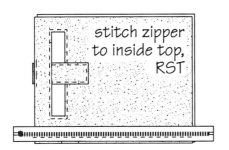

stitch zipper to inside top, RST

c. Stitch other side of zipper tape to top edge of inside-bottom unit in same manner.

d. Turn to right side. Finger-press seam allowances toward fabric; edge-stitch on both sides of zipper.

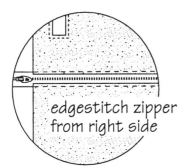

edgestitch zipper from right side

5. Make shoulder strap/loop strip

a. Fold shoulder strap/loop strip in half lengthwise, right sides together. Stitch, using a scant ⅜" seam allowance. Turn right side out. Press, positioning seam at side.

b. Cut an 8½" length from tube for loop strip. Edgestitch two 1¾" rectangles,

beginning ¾" from each end (these will become the loops).

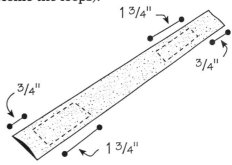

1 ³/₄"

³/₄"

³/₄"

1 ³/₄"

6. Join panels

a. Baste outside lining to outside fabric panel close to edges, wrong sides together.

b. Mark stitching line 4⅛" from bottom edge of inside panel. Center inside over outside panel, wrong sides together (inside unit will be barely shorter at both ends). Pin in place. Stitch along marked line.

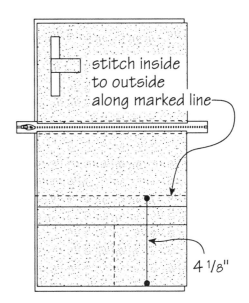

stitch inside to outside along marked line

4 ¹/₈"

c. Mark a line on right side of outside panel, 3½" from top edge. Position loop strip on fabric, with top edge just below marked line. Edgestitch loop strip to bag in three steps: from edge to beginning of first loop, between loops (pinch loop sections together to keep them free), and from remaining loop to remaining edge.

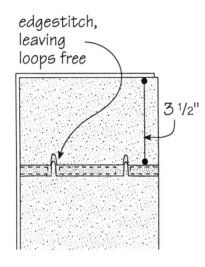

edgestitch, leaving loops free

3 ½"

7. Add closure and bind edges

a. Trim remaining hook-and-loop tape to 3" long. Position loop side on inside-top, centered, ⅜" from top raw edge; edgestitch. (*Note:* Fold outside panel out of the way.)

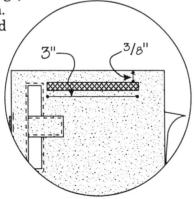

3"   ⅜"

b. Position hook side on outside-bottom, centered, 2½" from raw edge; edgestitch. (*Note:* Fold inside panel out of the way.)

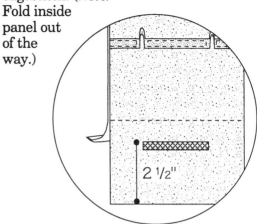

2 ½"

c. Gently curve top corners. (*Tip:* Use a juice glass to define curves.) Trim side edges even. (*Note:* Be sure zipper pull is within fabric area before trimming off ends.) Pin panels together at edges, easing outside fabric to fit. Baste, serge, or zigzag raw edges together.

d. Trim end of bias binding at a 45° angle (to reduce bulk); turn under ¼". Beginning in center of one long side, stitch binding to wallet from the inside, right sides together, using ¼" seam allowance.

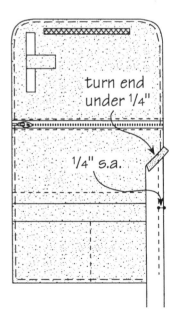

turn end under ¼"

¼" s.a.

To turn corners: Stitch to within ¼" of edge; lock and cut threads. Fold binding 45°, away from fabric.

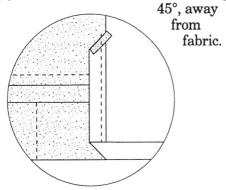

Fold again toward fabric, aligning edges. Resume stitching ¼" from both edges.

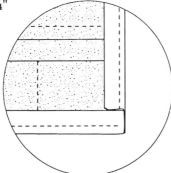

To end: Lap and stitch end of binding ½" beyond beginning fold. Trim at 45° angle. Trim off triangle.
Optional: Stitch ends of binding together invisibly.

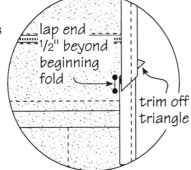

lap end
½" beyond beginning fold

trim off triangle

e. Wrap binding snugly over edges. Turn under raw edge of binding to leave ¼" showing on outside; pin. Edgestitch in place.

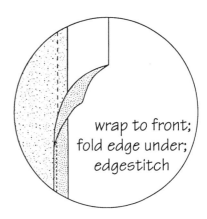

wrap to front; fold edge under; edgestitch

8. Finish bag

Trim ends of shoulder strap at a 45° angle. Thread ends through loops on top of bag; tie. Untie strap to slip wallet into a purse.

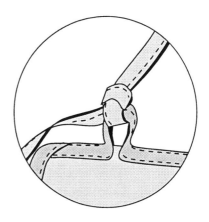

Note: If strap is too long, either cut off excess from one end or tie a loop at top of strap.

Options, Ideas & Variations...

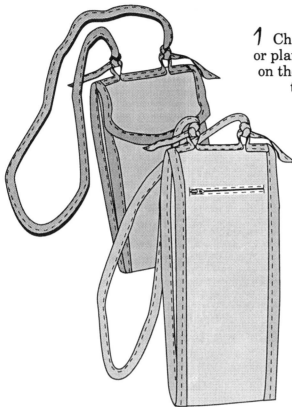

1 Change the size. How about a passport- or plane-ticket–size wallet? Add a zipper on the outside back so you can get to your travel documents without opening the entire wallet.

2 Use small brass snap-hooks instead of knots to attach the straps.

3 Close the bag and tab pocket with gripper snaps rather than hook-and-loop tape.

4 Customize the pockets. Mix and match zippered and open pockets to suit your particular needs. For instance, add a clear vinyl pocket to the inside to keep a driver's license or other I.D. in plain view.

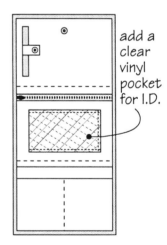

add a clear vinyl pocket for I.D.

Glossary

bias Any diagonal direction of fabric, but generally refers to the "true bias," 45° from the straight grain of fabric; a true bias edge does not ravel.

bodkin A tool for threading elastic through a casing; a safety pin is usually an adequate substitute.

casing A "tunnel," created by stitching two layers of fabric together with parallel lines of stitches, through which a cord or elastic is inserted.

center-release buckle A two-piece plastic buckle that opens by pressing down in the center.

clean-finish To prepare a raw edge so it will not ravel; common techniques are to overcast the edge with zigzag stitching or serging, to turn the edge under ¼" and stitch, and to trim the edge using pinking shears.

cording String or rope, widely available in home-dec departments; may be decorative or used to make welting.

denier A measure of the fineness of a silk, rayon, or nylon yarn; the higher the number, the thicker the fiber (and heavier the fabric).

ease To force a shorter piece of fabric to fit a longer one, by stretching the shorter and compressing the longer one.

edgestitch To straight-stitch as close

as possible to an edge, about ¹⁄₁₆"–⅛".

finger-press To flatten a seamline or fold using your fingers or fingernails.

fusible web An airy, nonwoven fabric that melts with heat and moisture, used to "glue" two pieces of fabric together; available in strips (on rolls) or as yardage (generally grouped with interfacings).

grain The direction of fibers in a piece of fabric; lengthwise grain runs parallel to the selvage; crosswise grain, perpendicular.

grommets Large metal eyelets.

home dec Commonly used abbreviation for "home decorating."

ladder buckle See *tabler buckle*.

parachute clip See *side-release buckle*.

piping A narrow folded strip of bias-cut fabric stitched into a seamline; can also be corded (for bags and home-dec, corded piping is usually called welting).

RSO Right side out.

RST Right sides together.

raw edge The cut edge of fabric.

s.a. Seam allowance.

seam allowance The width of fabric between a line of stitching and the edge.

sear A method of clean-finishing the raw edges of nylon or polypropylene by passing it through the base of a flame or cutting with a hot-knife tool.

selvage or **selvedge** The finished edges of fabric, as it comes from the mill.

serge To stitch with an overlock machine, also called a serger; serging stitches the seam and clean-finishes edges in one step; sergers most commonly stitch using three or four threads.

shoulder pad A flat piece of plastic or rubber or a small pad with slits at either end to thread webbing through; used to keep straps from slipping off shoulders. (*Note:* This is an entirely different animal from a garment shoulder pad!)

side-release buckle A two-piece plastic buckle that opens by squeezing the two sides; also called a parachute clip.

slider A rectangular piece of hardware with a center bar; used to allow one piece of webbing to slide over another, for adjusting length.

snaphook A plastic or brass hook that opens and closes with a spring mechanism, used for detachable shoulder straps; a "swivel snaphook" has a base that can turn 360° (use plain and swivel snaphooks interchangeably for most projects in this book).

stitch in the ditch To straight-stitch invisibly in the well of a seam, or next to a seamline, from the right side.

tabler buckle A rectangular piece of hardware with two slanting center bars and a rounded tab at one end; used to lock a piece of webbing by turning it back on itself; also called a double-bar buckle or a ladder buckle.

toggle A small, spring-loaded cylinder with a hole drilled through; used to secure drawstrings and laces.

topstitch To straight-stitch ⅜"–¼" from an edge; this is usually decorative, and often done with heavy ("topstitching") or specialty thread.

turn of the cloth The amount of fabric required to turn an edge; for thick fabrics and for turning over several layers of fabric this can be ¼" or more.

WSO Wrong side out.

WST Wrong sides together.

webbing A strong fabric tape used for handles and straps on bags; available in various widths, weights, and colors; most often made from nylon, polypropylene, or cotton.

web-ring A piece of hardware to which a snaphook attaches; a D-ring or Tri-Ring can be substituted.

welting Cording encased in a bias-cut strip of fabric, intended to be stitched into a seamline (on garments, this is called corded piping).

zigzag stitch A machine stitch in which the needle swings left-to-right as it moves forward.

Sources and Resources

Your selection of fabrics, notions, and findings appropriate for making bags may be limited in fabric stores. If so, check other types of local retailers (see "Where to Look for Fabric and Supplies" in the Introduction, pages x–xi). If you still can't find what you need locally, mail order is a good alternative. The following is a list of mail-order retailers that I know of; no doubt there are more. Check the classified advertisements in sewing publications like *Sew News* and *Threads* for other sources.

Atlantic cloth

Nancy's Notions
P.O. Box 683
Beaver Dam, WI 53916
(An extensive selection of sewing notions; call for free catalog or to order, 800-833-0690.)

Findings (beads, coins, etc.)

Stitch N Craft Wholesale Club
(a membership organization)
5634 West Meadowbrook Avenue
Phoenix, AZ 85031
(A large selection of sewing and crafts books, notions, and supplies, including beads and conchos, all at wholesale prices; send SASE for membership information.)

Tandy Leather Company
P.O. Box 791
Fort Worth, TX 76101
(A large selection of metallic hardware and findings, including beads and conchos; send for free catalog and listing of the retail and mail-order service center nearest you.)

Worldly Goods
848 Camino Del Pueblo
Bernalillo, NM 87004
(A wonderful selection of unusual and hard-to-find buttons, beads, amulets, coins, and jewelry supplies; friendly, personalized service; send $5 for catalog, refundable with purchase, or call 505-867-1303.)

Handles, clasps, snaps, etc.

Birch Street Clothing
P.O. Box 6901
San Mateo, CA 94403
(The truly superior Vario Plus snap kit complete with setting tools for many sizes of snaps, eyelets, and grommets; send $1 for catalog, or call 800-736-0854 to order.)

Clotilde
2 Sew Smart Way
B8031
Stevens Point, WI 54481-8031
(An extensive selection of sewing notions, including leather and chain handles, clasps, frames, and patterns; write or call for free catalog, 800-772-2891.)

Ghee's
2620 Centenary Boulevard
Building 3, Suite 205
Shreveport, LA 71104
*(Linda McGehee carries a wide
selection of purse patterns, frames,
and findings, as well as two wonderful books on surface design; send $1
for catalog.)*

G Street Fabrics
12240 Wilkins Avenue
Rockville, MD 20852
*(An exceptional variety of gold and
silver chain for handles; also grommets, snaps, and other notions; call
800-333-9191 to order.)*

My Sunday Best
2313 Lytal Lane
Edmond, OK 73013
*(Leather handles; send for free
catalog.)*

Stitch N Craft Wholesale Club
*(Frames, clasps, snaps, chain, suede
lace, and patterns; see information
on page 129.)*

Tandy Leather Company
*(Leather handles, clasps, snaps, D-
rings; see information on page 129.)*

Insulating fabrics

*(Most of the outdoor-fabric sources
listed on pages 131–132 also carry
Thinsulate.)*

Nancy's Notions
*(Thinsulate, Warm Winter; see
information on page 129.)*

Laminated fabrics & supplies

*(Check first in the home-dec depart-
ment at your fabric store.)*

Britex Fabrics
146 Geary Street
San Francisco, CA 94108
*(A wide selection of fine fabrics,
including laminates; write or call
for information, 415-392-2910.)*

Field's Fabrics by Mail
1695 Forty-fourth Street SE
Grand Rapids, MI 49508-5001
*(A wide selection of fine fabrics,
including laminates; write or call
for information, 616-455-4570.)*

My Sunday Best
*(Laminated yardage and kits; send
$3 for swatch sheet and catalog; see
information at left.)*

Stitches 'n Stuff
Route 2, Box 224
Elmore City, OK 73035
*(Fab-Lam for laminating fabric;
send SASE for information; 405-
788-4478.)*

Leather & suede, natural

Britex Fabrics
*(A wide selection of fine fabrics,
including natural leather; see information above.)*

Iowa Pigskin Expressions
9185-210 Street
Walcott, IA 52773
*(A complete selection of pigskin
leathers; write for information.)*

Stitch N Craft Wholesale Club
(Garment leathers and suede lace; see information on page 129.)

Tandy Leather Company
(A complete selection of garment and accessory leathers, plus metallic hardware and suede lace; catalogs often include free patterns for accessories and jewelry; see information on page 129.)

Leather & suede, synthetic

Britex Fabrics
(A wide selection of fine fabrics, including Ultrasuede, Ultrasuede Light, and Ultraleather; see information on page 130.)

Classic Cloth
34930 US 19 N
Palm Harbor, FL 34684
(A selection of fine fabrics, including Ultrasuede, Ultrasuede Light, and Ultraleather; also Ultrasuede trims, fringe, and braid; send $5 for swatch set, refundable with purchase; 800-237-7739.)

Field's Fabrics by Mail
(A selection of fine fabrics, including Ultrasuede, Ultrasuede Light, and Ultraleather; send $10 for set of over 75 swatches, refundable with purchase, to address on page 130; 800-67-ULTRA.)

G Street Fabrics
(A wide selection of fine fabrics, including Ultrasuede, Ultrasuede Light, and Ultraleather; also Ultrasuede trims and fringe; send

$10 for complete swatch set, refundable with purchase, to address on page 130; 800-333-9191.)

Michiko's Creations
P.O. Box 4313
Napa, CA 94558
(Ultrasuede, Ultrasuede Light, and Ultraleather; also a wide selection of gorgeous traditional Japanese papers and fabrics; excellent service; send $10 for 100 swatches; send SASE for information.)

Donna Salyers' Fabulous-Furs
700 Madison Avenue
Covington, KY 41011
(Fabu-Leather, a top-quality synthetic leather that has pretty much replaced Ultraleather; write or call for a free catalog, 606-291-3300.)

Outdoor fabrics & hardware (webbing, toggles, zippers, etc.)

Birch Street Clothing
(Toggles and zippers; see information on page 129.)

Britex Fabrics
(A wide selection of fine fabrics, including Cordura and Ultrex; see information on page 130.)

Clotilde
(A limited selection of webbing and snaphooks, plus dress-weight zipper-by-the-yard; see information on page 129.)

Field's Fabrics by Mail
(A selection of fine fabrics, including Supplex and Ultrex; see information on page 130.)

Frostline USA Inc.
19th Floor
11 Penn Plaza
New York, NY 10001
*(Fabrics, webbing, and hardware;
also kits and patterns; for free
catalog call 800-KITS USA.)*

The Green Pepper
3918 West First Avenue
Eugene, OR 97402
*(An exceptional selection of outdoor
fabrics, hardware, zippers, toggles,
cording, and webbing in a wide
range of weights, colors, and sizes;
also patterns; send $2 for catalog;
503-345-6665.)*

Nancy's Notions
*(Limited selection of toggles, web-
bing, and buckles, plus dress-weight
zipper-by-the-yard; see information
on page 129.)*

Outdoor Wilderness Fabrics
16195 Latah Drive WTW
Nampa, ID 83651
*(A complete line of fabrics for out-
door clothing and recreational gear;
also hardware, buckles, zippers,
webbing, and patterns; send $4 for
full set of fabric samples, including
all available colors; write or call for
free price list, 208-466-1602.)*

Seattle Fabrics
3876 Bridge Way N
Seattle, WA 98103
*(An exceptional selection of outdoor
fabrics, hardware, zippers, toggles,
cording, and webbing in a wide
range of weights, colors, and sizes;
also patterns and books; send $3 for
price list, refundable with purchase.)*

Shaker Workshops
P.O. Box 1028
Concord, MA 01742
*(A colorful selection of heavy-duty
100% cotton webbing ("chair tape")
in 1" and ⅝" widths, plus beautiful
Shaker-style furniture, kits, and
accessories; send $1 for catalog and
webbing samples.)*

Sundrop Outerwear Textiles Inc.
140-1140 Austin Avenue
Coquitlam, B. C. V3K 3P5 Canada
*(An exceptional selection of outdoor
fabrics, hardware, zippers, toggles,
cording, and webbing in a wide
range of weights, colors, and sizes;
also patterns; send $2 for catalog,
refundable with purchase.)*

The Rain Shed
Department NR
707 Northwest Eleventh Street
Corvallis, OR 97330
*(An exceptional selection of outdoor
fabrics, hardware, zippers, toggles,
and webbing, in a wide range of
colors and sizes; also patterns; an
excellent catalog with lots of sewing
tips; send $1 for catalog.)*

Tapestry fabrics

Britex Fabrics
*(A wide selection of fine fabrics,
including tapestries; see information
on page 130.)*

G Street Fabrics
*(A wide selection of fine fabrics,
including tapestries; see information
on page 130.)*